CONFLICT IN DI
Plays for Educatio

THE

SOCIAL

CONFLICT

Introductory notes by
JOHN HODGSON and
AUDREY COLDRON

There's No Room for You Here for a Start –
Henry Livings

The Kitchen – *Arnold Wesker*

Soldier, Soldier – *John Arden*

Methuen Educational Ltd

LONDON · TORONTO · SYDNEY · WELLINGTON

109217

First published 1972
by Methuen Educational Ltd, 11 New Fetter Lane, London EC4

© *1972 Introductory notes by John Hodgson and Audrey Coldron*

THERE'S NO ROOM FOR YOU HERE FOR A START
© 1964 Henry Livings
First published in 1964 in a collection
Kelly's Eye and Other Plays
by Henry Livings, in the series *Methuen's Modern Plays*
(Methuen & Co Ltd)

THE KITCHEN © 1961 Arnold Wesker
First published in an original and shorter version
by Penguin Books 1960.
This version was first published by Jonathan Cape 1961.

SOLDIER, SOLDIER © 1967 John Arden
First published in 1967 in a volume called
Soldier, Soldier and Other Plays
by John Arden, in the series *Methuen's Modern Plays*
(Methuen & Co Ltd)

Printed in Great Britain
by Fletcher and Son Ltd, Norwich

SBN 423 80250 X

Contents

General Introduction

Each of these three plays was written by an author with a keen social awareness and concern. All three authors were born before the war (in 1928, 1930 and 1932 respectively), grew up and went to school during the war and faced the post-war world with a sense of renewed vision about values and attitudes in society. Of the three, Arnold Wesker is the man with the strongest social and political mission; Henry Livings focuses attention on social misfits of society and John Arden sets out on a quest for a viable morality, not to present us with it, but to leave us with the questions and problems involved even in formulating it.

In *There's No Room for You Here for a Start* we see the kind of social conflicts which arise within the home, the adjustment and moral adjustment of individuals in the domestic situation. These people are then placed in conflict with the representative of the larger community—the local council. The family have walled themselves round with a nine-foot hedge but the authorities want to reduce this to a mere two feet. In a sense it is wrong to say that Miss Thynne has put the hedge there—in fact she has rather let it happen but now that it is part of her property we resent the intrusion from the Town Clerk.

The Kitchen by Arnold Wesker takes us to the world of work and shows us the conflicts which arise as a result of people who are caught up in the industrial machine and not allowed the opportunity to dream and attempt to fulfil their dreams. Wesker points out the difficulties of survival of the human spirit in such an environment and urges his characters to break out from the destructive nature of their employment.

In *Soldier, Soldier* we find another kind of conflict. This time we are given a community which already exists more or less harmoniously and see the problems which occur when an un-conducive force in the nature of a soldier makes his appearance. We find the characters pressed in by the powers of the society in the first play; in the second we witness some of the struggles within it and in the last we have a force which attempts to dislodge the structure.

Two of the plays were first written for television and Wesker's *The Kitchen* was later made into a film. Each of the plays employs a different approach and style of writing. Livings uses great economy in the dialogue. While he writes with a sense of the vernacular he retains a definite feeling for shape of sentence and interplay of dialogue. Arnold Wesker's prose is more expansive and he rarely loses an opportunity of presenting and underlining the social importance of what is being said. He tends to have a clear message and to declare it unashamedly. John Arden is the most complex of the writers here represented. Throughout his work he says he finds that very often what he has to say can best be said in verse. Here he is experimenting to see if verse is a possibility as a means of play-writing for the small screen. He is modest about his achievements and believes that his writing comes off best when he uses verse which is colloquial and humorous. He is less happy about the attempts he makes to write verse in a more lyrical mood. It is worth comparing his brand of comedy and approach with that of Henry Livings. Arnold Wesker is a more serious, perhaps even earnest writer and rarely allows much scope for comedy, though certainly in his earlier plays he keeps a vigour and vitality in his work which sustains our interest.

These plays can be enjoyed in reading but their full qualities will best be appreciated if they are acted at some point as well. Enjoying them in a three-dimensional form will raise many more points about character, about style of writing and about ideas. The human relationships unfolded through the social conflicts will be understood more fully when 'lived' through in the acting of the text or in the improvisational approach related to the text.

None of these dramas needs elaborate decor before it can be acted. In fact, it could be agreed that such is the continuity required by each of these that too much attention to setting could easily weigh down the action.

The demand is on the actors, in both understanding their parts and in interpreting this in performance. The business contains an element of paradox: by attempting to act out the plays the understanding grows, by reading the texts and arguing about the meaning and attitudes the interpretation develops into a more effective performance.

Before each play there is an introduction which sets out some information about the author and a discussion of his place in the theatre today. The theme and the characters in the particular play are discussed and suggestions for ways in which the piece can be presented in a small space are developed. At the end of the volume there are hints for further points of discussion and improvisations which could be explored and expanded in the context of the plays. Some indication of rehearsal methods in which larger groups could be involved in small cast plays is given.

Introduction to

THERE'S NO ROOM
FOR YOU HERE FOR A START
Henry Livings

THE PLAYWRIGHT AND HIS WORK

There is a warm, amiable outgoing quality about both Henry Livings and his writings. When you talk to him you can see in his bright eyes that you are with a shrewd observer. But he doesn't look through you because the expression is friendly. He's a lively story-teller. His keen wit and ability at impersonation easily sustain interest. He can be amused by anyone but reserves his criticism for those who adopt superior and authoritative airs.

He says that even when he was at school he was aware that something in the state of things was wrong—though at that time he was unable to decide what it was. He had been to grammar school in the suburbs of Manchester where he was born in 1929. His father worked at Dunlops. The only person who really captured his interest was the Spanish master and here already we can see his sympathy for the underdog. This Spanish teacher was looked down upon by the other teachers because he didn't have a degree. But he had enough enthusiasm to inspire the young Henry Livings to want to take Hispanic studies at the university. The headmaster of the grammar school told Henry Livings that he was disappointed that he had not gained a place at Oxford or Cambridge. Instead Henry Livings went for a couple of years to Liverpool University.

There he took part in the dramatics—he acted Faustus among other parts but he left Liverpool without a degree and went into the R.A.F. On demob he did all kinds of jobs from washing up to being a first-class cook, as well as acting with a variety of repertory companies in different parts of the country.

He began writing at school—an epic poem—and again while at Liverpool University but it wasn't until he was out of work for three weeks (after he had damaged an ankle), that he felt he had the opportunity of devoting himself to writing. The director, Denis Carey, showed some interest and this encouraged him to try a half-hour television play. However, when he showed this to Gerald Glaister who had produced a TV play in which Henry had just acted, Glaister said TV plays needed to be of an hour's length and encouraged him to try again. A month later a television play called *Jack's Horrible Luck* was on the producer's desk and provided Livings with enough money to devote himself to another few months' writing. His first play to reach the public was *Stop It Whoever You Are*, at the Arts Theatre in London in 1961. This received a certain amount of controversial notice and the BBC who had up to then held on to Livings' TV drama without showing it, now were encouraged to bring it out of cold storage and put it into rehearsal. Henry Livings had emerged as a playwright of notoriety!

In February 1963, Granada TV presented *There's No Room for You Here for a Start*.

Henry Livings pays tribute to the influence of Joan Littlewood upon his writing and appreciation of theatre. He had worked with her Company, Theatre Workshop, between 1956 and 1958; 'what she gave me', he says, 'was her ability to analyse theatre, to break down a theatrical situation into its essences! Of course it developed from Stanislavsky* but she suddenly made his ideas come alive for me'.

He applied this analysis to his writing: 'I broke down the stories into units of about ten minutes each—about as long, I reckoned, as you can hold a new situation clearly and totally in

* Stanislavsky, the great Russian director and author of *An Actor Prepares*.

mind. Each unit I then tried to lay against what went before and what followed, so that the audience would be fresh each time and yet carry an accumulating imaginative world along towards the end and completion of the play'.

In plays like *Big Soft Nelly* and *Eh!* he shows considerable disregard for plot by presenting a series of incidents which show traits of character. His idea of ten minute units is seen very clearly in his brilliant Pongo plays—a series of brief sketches each showing an incident involving the same central character, Sam Pongo.

Henry Livings has continued to write for both stage and television and still acts mainly for radio and television, though with Alex Glasgow he presents live performances of Northern Drift—items acted from the works of writers in the North who share a similar conviction and passion for things which, while hilariously funny, retain an element of the sad.

It may be useful to read the play at this point before continuing with the introduction.

THEME AND CHARACTERS

Henry Livings, then, often uses the conventions of farce to convey ideas which are serious. In *There's No Room for You Here for a Start* we have a play about Len Milne, a rather mad fellow who comes to find lodgings with Lily Thynne. Both of these people in a way call upon our feelings of pathos: Len has a battered steel hook where his left hand should be and about his mentality he says, 'That's a big lump o'bone I got there.' (*His head*) (p. 41). Lily because of her early childhood experience when she was assaulted by her own father has remained cold and afraid and 'I was took away and put with an auntie', she tells Len (p. 47).

Yet in both of them there is compassion and affection. For all his ability to frighten, Len is really a very gentle, careful soul. Lily is scared at the beginning when Len gets his iron hook stuck in the letter box, but he soon wins her round with his concern and thoughtfulness. He drops his ash on the carpet but immediately is anxious to sweep it up. Then when he sits down to his stew he apologizes about his manners and quickly Lily reassures him without a hint of patronizing; 'Go on, you eat as best you can; it's no shame' (p. 26).

The social conflict is already there seen in the letter on the mantelpiece. The Town Clerk has written to order that their nine foot untidy hedge be cut to twenty-four inches. The plot is indeed simple and the relationship between the characters may at first seem corny but Livings manages to take us beyond the surface in our regard for the people and reaches out from the immediate situation to the more universal.

The invasion of privacy by officials is something which concerns us all. Rules are made for the mass; often when the letter of the law is applied there is considerable disregard for both individual liberty and feeling. Absurd though the situation is, it nevertheless is not fictitious. Henry Livings, as a boy, lived in a house which was similar to that in the play and his hedge he says was similarly threatened. As I write I am reminded of a report in today's paper that the council men at Stratford-upon-Avon have ruthlessly cut back hedges which surrounded the place where Shakespeare is said to have died. Instead of picturesque shaped yew hedges they have left an unsightly black skeleton because the green overlapped the pavement by a foot!

Because of his regard for Lily, Len undertakes her protection and with delightful touches of absurdist comedy he keeps the council men at bay, first by appearing to them in his pyjamas at all hours of the morning and then by frightening them off with a shot-gun. The officials whom Livings shows us are humorously pompous and skilfully sketched in their cowardliness. We derive the same kind of amusement from seeing them scarper in the van at the sight of the shot-gun as we enjoy when the posh lady steps from her car into a puddle in a Charlie Chaplin film. We are even more delighted when we see the simple and contrite Len up before the police sergeant and witness his release without charge.

Each incident adds something to our understanding of Len. Livings says that he doesn't wish us to let our sympathy come easily for his 'heroes'. Yet although we may have a few prejudices with regard to Len, we do feel on his side almost as soon as Lily does. When we meet Len's mother we are pleased that she has difficulty in finding him. Her overpowering nature and blunt simplicity almost make us want to hide with him. It is Len's lack of affection which makes him all the more understanding and loving towards Lily.

Even Mary, who senses that Len might steal away the love which she enjoys from Lily, seems to come round in the end. At least she acts with wit and a nice sense of perspective when she informs the council men that neither Miss Thynne nor Mr. Milne are in—and then gives them permission to cut the hedge.

Harold remains obstinately against Len. He has none of Len's sensitivity—all he can register is fear. When the golf clubs and gun almost fall on him from the loft, all he can believe is that he has encountered a lunatic. Actually his attempt at superiority only adds to the fun and after his show at a fight with Len and Mrs. Milne's rebuke, he can only echo Len with, 'I've had about enough of everything' (p. 60).

The workmen also, find themselves unable to know how to deal with Len. First he shoots at them, then he helps them cut the very hedge he has fought over and even shares his troubles with them. There is a resilience in Len and even though he declares, 'that's the finish of me in this house!' (p. 64), he goes on hacking the hedge.

ACTING AND PRODUCTION

This play could be acted either as a television sequence or a play for the stage. If closed circuit television is available, a series of simple interiors could be set up and one exterior with the hedge. It may be easier to use cine cameras and actual location shots with hand held equipment.

Henry Livings did offer to rewrite this play in a stage version, but it seemed that it would be perhaps more interesting to have this original version, in order to see how the writer thinks in terms of visual as well as verbal comedy. Having read the version here it might be useful to ask what changes would be necessary to prepare it for straight acting. The main differences would of course be in terms of setting and style of presentation. Things are presented in a very realistic fashion on television. In the stage version of the play we could concentrate more upon the characters and the interplay of personality.

One or two simple props would be useful for classroom acting. Something to represent the front door would help and this could be placed so as to divide the acting area into two sections—inside the house and the garden. Upstairs could be suggested by a short flight of steps leading out of sight and most of the upper floor activity could be done by voices and noises off. The scene between Lily and Len in the bedroom could perhaps be played downstairs on the sofa.

The hedge seems important. In both this play and Livings' *Stop It Whoever You Are*, the hedge seems to have a symbolic

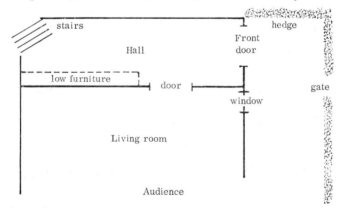

significance—it sums up a great many of the privacies and simple rights of the individual. But it could be represented by a more realistic piece of scenery. The cutting only takes place at the end of the play and the snap of the shears or the swish of the billhook will establish that the action has begun. Items of low furniture will help to mark off the edges of the room. The van can be indicated with horn and engine sounds off-stage.

Various improvisations will help in building up the characters. Scenes could be played out between Len and his mother, Lily and Mary, Lily and Harold, before the acting of the play begins. There could also be scenes imagined at the Town Clerk's and Borough Surveyor's offices to help make clear the attitudes and characters. Simple items of costume will help, as will properties like golf clubs and the gun, and these too will no doubt suggest a whole series of improvisations in deciding how they first came into the house.

Once the characterizations have been thought about in this way, it will become easier to act them in the context of the play. Notice that the dialogue is very naturalistic and straight-forward. Something of this directness of expression should be attempted in improvisations. Care should be taken not to strain after the comedy—the playwright has made this clear and in acting it out, it is best to play the situation sincerely, believing in the characters. Although there is much of farce in the play, there is also a great deal of sympathy and understanding.

Look out for the Stanislavsky-type units that Livings spoke about in the way he conceived his plays. Understanding of these will assist understanding of the structure and build of the production. One sequence will flow into another and the general pace can be kept rising to the end of sequence 5. At 6 the pace is steadier and from this point moves firmly to the end. Keep a look out for the points of tenderness and pathos—there is no need to make them sentimental; the surrounding comedy should sustain the vitality.

Something of Livings' own personality should be seen in the acting out of his plays. He himself is a lively man of passionate feeling but he manages also to retain a relaxed and easy-going quality amidst it all.

There's No Room
for You Here for a Start

HENRY LIVINGS

This play was first presented by Granada TV on 8 February 1963.

1. *The Farm: daytime: studio.*

We see perspectives of a huge, shopless, publess, treeless council estate. Wide streets lined with heaps of clay where grass verges are planned. A large hoarding with a crest and 'W.C.C. Housing and Development Dept.' which announces that 'This site was set aside on the suggestion of H.R.H. The Duke of WXXXX as a children's playground. No tipping. No trespassers. No children. By order. Town Clerk.'

Now a row of neat symmetrical houses surrounded by hedges exactly two foot high. Suddenly the neat privet is replaced by the towering swaying tangled and rampant mess of a hedge round 'The Farm'. There is a little may here and there. We can just see through to the whitewashed brick walls, the mouldering window-frames with clean curtains and the painted corrugated-iron roof: but only just, because the narrow garden is choked with enormous weeds. Rank hollyhocks and sunflowers and tall grasses.

LEN MILNE, *a bony-faced greying man in flat cap and old raincoat, with his left hand in his pocket, is peering from the footpath in at the house. He moves restlessly to get a better view.*

Inside the front room, LILY THYNNE, *buxom with round dark eyes and a touch of grey in her dark hair and only slightly more eyebrows than is downright beautiful, sitting, a little tensely, having a cup of tea; and* MARY, *about twenty, strident strongly built, the same type physically as* LILY, *who is her adoptive mother, but plain. They are talking in whispers.* MARY *is irritated.*

MARY. Well, good heavens, Mother, how long's he been there?

LILY. Ever since he first came. Look (*Indicates the mirror which gives her a view of the front garden.*) he's at it again.

MARY. He's a lunatic.

LILY. No, he isn't. I won't have you saying that when you don't know.

MARY. Dodging about, and staring at the house through the hedge. Shall I go and tell him to go away?

LILY. No.

MARY. Don't you want him to go?

LILY. You never know.

MARY. Well, go to the box and phone a policeman.

LILY. Oh, don't be ridiculous; he'll go shortly.

MARY. I'm being ridiculous! D'you want him to go or don't you?

LILY. There's something funny about him. You have to pity such men.

MARY. Oh, I give up. What time's our Harold coming for his tea?

LILY. Look! He's coming in again! I shan't answer. I heard him looking through the letter-box last time.

MARY. I said is our Harold coming back for his tea tonight?

> LILY *goes out into the hall, where* LEN *is scratching at the letter-box. She bends over and looks him straight in the eye.*

LILY. Boo!

> LEN *jumps. His left hand, which is a battered steel hook, slips through and catches on the inside of the door. He extricates it.*

LEN. Extremely sorry, miss!

> LILY *screams and runs back into the front room.*

LILY. Oh, my God, daughter, he's got something stuck in the letter-box!

MARY (*rises defensively*). The beast.

> MARY *rushes out to the hall and opens the front door.* LEN *is standing anxiously outside, left hand in his raincoat pocket.*

You'll get arrested, you will.

LEN. Yes, well. I'm extremely sorry I made you scream just now, miss.

MARY. That's just where you're wrong. I didn't.

LEN. Oh no, I just heard you scream. I'm very very sorry about that.

MARY. That was my mother.

LEN. I didn't know you was married. I got my hand stuck, see.

LILY (*off*). I know it wasn't!

MARY. He says it was his hand, Mother.

LILY (*off*). I know it wasn't!

MARY (*to* LEN). Lies aren't going to help, you dirty pig.

LEN. Only I came about the card.

> *After a moment's hesitation* MARY *goes back into the front room.* LEN *follows.*

MARY. He says he came about the card.

LILY. I know what he came about.

MARY (*to* LEN). There's no room here for you for a start.

LEN. Yes, well, you see (*To* LILY.), I had a thought after you said the room had been taken (*To* MARY.) – no, don't stop me; I been thinking about this (*To* LILY.) – maybe you got a room like (*To* MARY.) – no, don't stop me; I gotta finish this now (*To* LILY.) – just anywhere, no bed, nothing; I'm not bothered, only I been wandering about, see; you get tired, proper palace you got here, an't you? I mean, it's clean.

MARY. You've got a cheek.

LEN. Perhaps I could just have a look at the room? That's if it isn't taken.

LILY. What's that you've got on your left hand?

LEN. That's just my hand.

LILY. Show me.

> LEN *shows her his hook. She shudders. He puts it back in his pocket.*)

LEN. I get a bit embarrassed about it; like it's unusual, isn't it? What with thinking where's my hand got to, and the look of the steel where flesh ought to be, people get a funny feeling, I think. But it's handy. (*Takes out a cigarette and lights it with one hand.*) I'd be glad if I could see the room.

LILY. Don't ever show me that again.

LEN. No, no, no. That's something personal to me.

LILY. Terms are two guineas a week.

She ushers him towards the stairs.

LEN. That'll suit me. Which way do I go?

LILY. I'll show you. (*She leads the way upstairs.*) I expect you'll want to be by yourself, won't you?

LEN. Oh, as much as possible. Where will you be very likely if I want to ask you anything?

LILY (*indicating the first door on the landing*). My brother sleeps there.

LEN. Oh yes.

She opens the third, and last door, and leaves him.

It looks very nice. I'll take it, missis.

LILY (*as she descends the stairs*). The lav's out the back and you can get water in the kitchen. (*She goes back in the front room.*) You know I should have asked three guineas. I meant to.

MARY. Don't talk to me – you're as mad as he is – we should have a row.

LILY. I shall be all right with him. It's better to have a man about the place.

MARY. What's our Harold if he isn't a man?

LILY. That two guineas and my mornings, I shan't have to ask anybody.

We hear the back door open and close.

MARY. There's our Harold.

LILY. Anyway, he's no need to stay for ever. He said he was a wanderer . . . he looked tired to me. There's plenty men like that: up roots and away.

We see HAROLD *in the scullery, sluicing himself at the sink. He is a little older than* LILY, *stocky, with a rosy clown's face that falls easily into a great grin. He takes his tea off the pan where it has been keeping hot and takes it into the kitchen, where the table is laid.* LILY *comes through from the front with the teapot and pours him some.* MARY *comes in.*

MARY. I'm going now, Mother. Hallo, Harold.

LILY. Don't stay away too long, darling.

MARY. I don't think I'd better. (*To* HAROLD *as she puts her coat on.*) Not been working too hard, our Harold?

HAROLD. Oh, steady, darling, steady. How's things at the hostel?

MARY. Fine, except I do most of the Matron's work as well.

LILY. You work too hard, Mary, at that hostel.

HAROLD. You're like me, fond of work.

HAROLD *is staggered by the appearance of* LEN *in the door to the hall. There is a brief pause, nobody is prepared for this.*

MARY. Good-bye, Mother; good-bye, Harold.

MARY *goes out by the back door.* LILY *retreats to the scullery.*

LEN. She's taken against me, your daughter.

HAROLD. How d'you do.

LEN. How d'you do. You live here, too?

HAROLD. It's my sister's house!

LEN (*addressing* LILY). Could I have such a thing as a brush, missis?

LILY (*coming in with a jug of hot water*). She's not really my daughter.

LEN. Miss.

LILY. What for? Is it not clean enough, the room?

LEN. Only some cigarette ash fell off my cigarette, see. I was making for the fireplace, holding it up, you know the way you do when you've left it too long. (*Holds up his cigarette to demonstrate. There is ash on it now.*) Only it had got all curved, it wasn't *secure*, see . . . I hope you don't mind my putting my end in the fire here? Well, damn me, it's happened again. It's a dirty stinking habit smoking and that's a fact. (*Rubs ash into carpet with his shoe.*)

HAROLD. What's your job?

LEN. I got a job nights. Good job. I shan't be no bother, you see. Engineering.

HAROLD. You weren't bothering me as it was.

LILY *brings* LEN *a dustpan and brush.*

LEN. And perhaps an ashtray?

She finds him a large one on the mantelpiece. LEN *goes out.* LILY *sits in an arm-chair by the fire.* HAROLD *clears his dirty crocks off the table to the scullery, seeing a letter on the mantelpiece as he passes. As he returns he picks up the letter and sits to read it, pouring himself a cup of tea. He opens the letter, spreads it with both hands on the table and reads stolidly.* LILY *watches with a show of indifference and reluctantly* HAROLD *gets up and takes his cup to the scullery, gets his jacket from behind the back door and goes out.* LILY *gets up and goes to replace the lace covers on the sugar and milk put a plate over the remaining bread and butter, and dust off the crumbs into her hand. She reads the letter without picking it up, and we read it with her.*
Dear Sir,

It has been laid down in Council that all perimeter hedges shall be 2 feet (24 inches) high. Although your property is not directly the responsibility of the authority, the Council must warn you that you are bound by the by-laws and regulations of the Council, and that your

original guarantee of tenure must depend on your compliance with decisions taken by the Council for the benefit
of the entire Estate.

Should you encounter any difficulty in reducing the
hedge to its proper height the Parks and Gardens Super-
visor has instructions to attend to it at your convenience.

In order to reduce administrative costs, this letter must
be taken as a final warning.

Your Obedient Servant,
(TOWN CLERK).

*LEN has reappeared in the door with the dustpan and brush
in one hand and the other in his pocket. LILY jumps as he
speaks.*

LEN. I wanted to return this. I done the sweeping, thank you.

LILY. Oh! Oh I thought I was alone in the house. Ouf, how
terrible.

LEN. Oh well, you an't, are you? What's more, you don't want
to be and that's a fact. I'm just going out for a bite and then
work, me, so don't you worry.

*She has half a mind to show him the letter and she diddle-
daddles.*

LILY. There's some tea in the pot if you'd like some.

LEN. Yes, I would, miss.

   LILY goes to the scullery for the pot.

And anyway there's your brother.

LILY (*returning*). I could do you a bite to eat if you like.

*She picks up the letter and stands helplessly before him,
waiting to be asked about it.*

LEN. That'd be a terrible nuisance, I shouldn't wonder.

LILY. It's ready now. And hot. Stew.

LEN. That'd be very welcome, I'm sure.

LILY flaps the letter briefly down on the table and goes into the scullery for his food. We hear her sigh painfully. LEN goes to the scullery door and looks at her. He comes back and peeks at the letter without picking it up.

Your Obedient Servant . . . Town Clerk.

LILY glances from the letter to him as she re-enters with the stew and a knife and fork. She lays the things ready for him, picks up the letter and goes to sit by the fire again, not looking at him. Hesitantly, he sits. He turns away and unscrews his hook to replace it with a fork. He starts to eat. She gets up, holding the letter to her, and crosses to stand by him. He looks up guiltily, his loaded fork-hand poised. He hastily shoves the fork, forkful and all, into his jacket pocket, instinctively, guarding his plate of stew with his right hand.

I'd no intention for you to see that. Sorry, miss. Only you see how I'm fixed now? (*He only has the knife in his right hand with which to eat.*) You must excuse my ways. I'm used to it rougher, see. Could I perhaps have a spoon?

LILY. What is it? It's not what it was before.

LEN. Only an old fork, miss.

LILY. You don't have to keep missing me.

LEN. No, well, I won't.

LILY. Go on, you eat as best you can; it's no shame.

He takes out the fork and begins to pick fluff off the food on it. LILY looks on with morbid fascination.

LEN. No, only I get a bit embarrassed about it. Funny old fork, isn't it? I got odd things off the National Health just recently (*Jingles his jacket pocket.*), but I get on fine with my own bits and pieces what I had made by a mate. I got a proper menagerie in here. Like I always say, I'm funny-looking, but I'm armless. There, that nearly had you smiling.

LILY (*wanly, as she returns to her seat*). Oh, you.

LEN. That's right, sit you down where you don't see my hand.

Perhaps I'll think of something else laughable after a while. You don't mind me talking familiar, do you?

She doesn't answer. He stares straight before him, and then tries to speak. But it only comes out as a strangled stammer.

I . . . I . . . I . . .

He gives up and goes back to gobbling his stew. LILY *watches this performance out of the corner of her eye. Then she puts the letter on the mantelpiece.*

Oh, you've had a letter, have you?

LILY. Yes.

LEN. That's nice. 'Course I'm not really armless, you know. It's just the hand.

LILY. Where's all your things?

LEN. Wha?

LILY. Luggage.

LEN. I got them at this place I work. They're all right there, and I hadn't nowhere else at the time, see.

LILY. Oh dear, oh dear, oh dear. Dirty rotten lot.

LEN. That's right. I'm going now. I don't want to be late for work. Beg your pardon.

LILY. No, no, it's not you; it's the letter. (LEN *stands bewildered.* LILY *pulls herself together and hands him the letter.*) Read that, will you, please, and tell me what it's all about?

LEN licks his fork clean, winds the letter between the prongs to hold it, takes out a pair of glasses, and reads, holding the letter well away.

LEN. It's a letter from the Town Clerk. See here, it says here at the top. And at the bottom. Making double sure. Says 'Dear Sir . . .' (*Looks at her and then reads on. Goes to the front room and contemplates the hedge. Comes back into the kitchen.*) Says your hedge's got to be two foot high. Or twenty-four inches, they don't mind which. That's about nine foot, that hedge.

LILY. But what does perimeter mean?

LEN. You got any other hedge?

LILY. No.

LEN. Then it means your hedge. (*Reads on.*)

LILY. But what are they going to do?

> LEN *puts the letter down on the table. During the next few exchanges we see the portentous threats at the end of the letter.*

LEN. The rest of it is just writing. Office writing. It says your hedge is too high.

LILY. Too high for what?

LEN. Too high for their liking.

LILY. But what should I do?

LEN. Tell you what, I'll cut it for you. Trim it nicely.

LILY. But . . . but . . . Oh, I don't know what to do.

LEN. You don't know altogether *what* you want, that's the truth of it, isn't it?

LILY. No, but I'm frightened of what's going to happen.

LEN. Now, you just see here. There's plenty fellers in offices got nothing better to do than write letters. Well, you got one; that's all there is to it. So don't you worry. I'm here, an't I?

LILY. What difference does that make?

LEN (*reassuring*). It doesn't make no difference at all. Your hedge, isn't it.

LILY. Well, yes.

LEN. So nobody's going to touch it if you don't want 'em to.

LILY. But what was the letter *for*?

LEN. That's just them complaining. They can complain, can't they? Got a perfect right?

LILY. But if they're going to be getting at me all the time . . . you know the way they send letters, like with radio licences . . .

LEN (*looks at her and then at the letter; reads*). 'This letter must be taken as a final warning.' Final. You won't have no more bother with them. They finished with you now. Like the newspapers with the football: 'Late night final' . . . the one before the last.

LILY. Oh, don't talk rubbish. They'll be sending men and heaven knows what.

LEN. Now, don't you get heated with me just because I'm one for finding a ray of comfort.

LILY. Oh, I'm sorry. You're so kind.

LEN. Yes. Well, I got fond of you, miss, that's what it is. (*Tries again to stammer something out.*) I . . . I . . . I . . .

LILY. What is it? You said that before.

LEN. Anyway, it's time I was off to work now. (*Abruptly.*) I'm very happy here.

LILY. Don't talk so soft; you've not been here above twenty minutes, not counting hanging around outside all afternoon.

LEN. You can be happy for twenty minutes, can't you? I'll tell you something now: soon as I got to thinking out there, after you said there wasn't no room for me, I got to thinking that you was very beautiful, beautiful, a very beautiful woman, very neat, and you got them eyes; anyway, the fact is, it's like this: I want to ask you to marry me and I hope you'll do the same for me.

LILY. Well, I never.

LEN. No, I didn't put that so good, did I? It's strange, because other times I'm a great old clatterer. You being a total stranger makes it harder, see. Never mind, you an't said nothing against me so far, so I'll be so bold as . . . (*He begins to stammer.*) as . . . as . . . I love you and that's a fact. And what's more I'm shaking all over.

There is a blank pause before he speaks again.

See, I do talk, don't I? I got a tongue, an't I? Thank you for me tea. I'll get off to work now.

He goes out abruptly. LILY *folds the letter and puts it*

behind the clock. She looks into the mirror, opening her eyes very wide to inspect them.
Fade out.

2. *It is now a week later. Saturday morning,* LEN *asleep in his room. His arm on the bedside table. Trousers across a chair. Evening paper on the floor. Large and menacing alarm clock clanging away on the mantelpiece next to the ashtray. Two large suitcases not emptied entirely . . . in fact, all the signs of a week's occupation in digs.*

Outside we see MRS MILNE, *a well-preserved old lady, peering through the hedge. She comes to the gate and hesitates before coming up the path to the front door.*
Inside the house HAROLD *is on the landing adjusting a very shaky pair of steps preparatory to climbing up to the trap-door which leads to the attic. We hear* MRS MILNE *knock at the front door.* HAROLD *looks round, feels money in his pocket. She knocks again. Reluctantly* HAROLD *goes down to the front door and opens it grudgingly, as to a commercial traveller or tallyman.*

MRS MILNE. Does Len Milne live here? Because I'm his mother.

HAROLD. Eh?

MRS MILNE. I want to know does Len Milne stay here? Are you Mr Thynne?

HAROLD. I am.

MRS MILNE. And Mrs Thynne advertised in Schofields' window for a lodger?

HAROLD. That'd be my sister and the room's taken; anyway, it was for a man . . . at least that's who's got it.

MRS MILNE. Who?

HAROLD. A man.

MRS MILNE. Len Milne?

HAROLD. How should I know? Only been here a week and he works nights.

MRS MILNE. That'll be him. Would you mind calling him?

HAROLD. I don't know as he's in.

MRS MILNE. Oh, my heavens, no and you won't know either, will you, until you call him?

 HAROLD tries to close the door. She pushes against it.

Oh! shutting the door on a poor old woman . . .

HAROLD. I'm not shutting the door, missis, I'm just closing it while I go and shout for him. (*Shuts the door and shouts upstairs.*) Hey! Hey! Are y'in?

 We see LEN in the bedroom open an eye and then close it again. HAROLD *opens the front door again.*

What did you say his name was?

MRS MILNE. Len Milne. Milne.

HAROLD (*shouts*). Len Milne! (*To her.*) No, he's not in. Happen he'll be back later. My sister's due back from work in about ten minutes, I should come back then.

MRS MILNE. How's he looking? Is she feeding him right? He'll have got thinner, I shouldn't be surprised.

HAROLD. Look, missis, what you don't seem to appreciate is I've got a step-ladder upstairs . . . If you'll just call back later. Good morning.

MRS MILNE. Yes, I will.

 She goes and HAROLD shuts the door. He goes upstairs. LEN is looking out of the landing window. He has pulled on his trousers over his pyjamas. He turns to HAROLD.

LEN. Was that her?

HAROLD. Well, of all the nellies . . . why didn't you answer?

LEN. You don't want to take too much notice of her. I left home, see. You doing a bit of work here? I'll give you a hand.

HAROLD. The ladder's a bad 'un; I was after my golf-clubs . . . I think they're up there somewhere. My dad was Scotch, you see. I thought I'd get a few bob on them.

LEN. Well, you hold on to the steps and let me climb up and have a look. (*He mounts the steps.*) Just ordinary golf-clubs, are they ? I'll soon find 'em. (*Wobble.*) This is what you call living dangerously, innit ?

HAROLD. Sooner you than me.

LEN. You just hold on tight. (*He gropes around in the attic with his hook.*) Dark, innit ? Here, I got hold of something. I got a bite.

He drags a shabby golfing bag to the edge of the trap. Dust, golf clubs, and a rusty shot-gun shower out in a dangerous hail. HAROLD *dodges to one side.*

D'you know how many there was supposed to be ?

There is dust and rust everywhere. HAROLD *glares angrily at* LEN. LEN *descends the ladder carefully, holding the bag on the end of his hook and offers it to* HAROLD, *who takes it and loads the clubs back in.* HAROLD *pushes the steps out of the way.*

There's something to be said for having a hook, see; if you'd had to do that yourself you'd have had to go all the way down and wash your hands, this minute. (*Wipes his right hand on his trousers.*) See, all I got to do is give my hand a bit of a dust. (*Blows the dust off it.*)

HAROLD (*meaning the gun*). That doesn't belong here; that's his gun. It ought to go back up.

LEN. It's been a good gun that has, only wants cleaning.

HAROLD. Aye, well, I'll put it back up later.

LEN. I'll clean it up for you; you let me have it and I'll have it right as rain in next to no time. (*Takes the gun.*) You'll be golfing and shooting just like your Scotch grandad, you see.

HAROLD *edges away down the stairs.* LEN *sights the gun with his right hand and takes imaginary shots.*

I was handy with one of these myself one time, you know.

HAROLD. Your mum said she'd be back.

LEN. That's right, I expect she will. Look, I don't want you to say anything to Lily, but them fellers from the Council was here again yesterday about the hedge. That's twice they woke me up in a morning just when I'm getting my rest. I had a word or two to say about that. 'Your hedge is too high by about seven foot', he says. 'Never you mind,' I says; 'that's none o' your business. She's not in.' Oh, I told 'em. (*Pot shots with the gun.*) Only don't worry Lily with it. I'll handle them if they chance it again. She don't want them getting at her, I do know that.

> HAROLD *continues to edge downstairs.* LEN *talks on.*

I'm about wild with getting no sleep two mornings, I can tell you, Harold. They got no consideration. Bang, bang, bang on the door, and all this hectoring, questions, questions.

> LEN *goes into the bedroom with the gun.*

It doesn't take two minutes o' that and you got a nasty feeling everyone's against you and somehow it's all your fault. Well, they can just watch out.

> LEN *re-emerges from the bedroom, no break in his flow of conversation, just as* HAROLD *is escaping through into the kitchen.*

Mind what I say, not a word to Lily. I'll tell her myself they called, but I shan't mention what they was threatening.

> LEN *goes calmly back into the bedroom.* HAROLD, *in the scullery, puts the bag of clubs outside the back door, gets a kettle and begins to fill it and put it on.*

MARY (*laughs*). Morning, Harold.

HAROLD. Hallo, love. (*Confidential.*) Hey, him upstairs, have you seen him?

MARY. The lodger? Well, yes. What's wrong with him?

> HAROLD *searches his mind.*

HAROLD. What's wrong with him? You may well ask. I just can't put it into words, but it's like you feel he's the sort of bloke you couldn't guarantee to make him see reason.

MARY (*cheerful*). Oh, get away with you, Harold. I grant you he's a bit peculiar . . .

HAROLD. Anyway, he dropped Dad's golf clubs on my head, and that's for certain.

MARY (*laughs*). He what? Oh, I'm sure it must have been an accident.

HAROLD (*after a sharp look at* MARY). I tell you, Mary, it's been a bad morning for me, Mary.

LILY *comes into the kitchen the front way.*

MARY (*to* LILY). Hallo, mum. How's Rodger the Lodger?

LILY. Now then, Mary, I'm sure you never learnt that sort of talk at the Orphanage nor from me.

MARY. Why, what did I say?

LILY (*she nearly repeats it*). Ooops! I let myself down there, didn't I?

MARY. Well, how is he?

LILY (*secretly*). Oh, he's quite a lad, he is.

MARY *looks absently at* HAROLD, *who has laid out tea-things and now goes out into the back garden.*

MARY. Well, he does seem to have made an impression in a week.

LILY. Mary, he's a perfect gentleman.

MARY. Oh, yes.

LILY. I see the kettle's on; let's have some tea.

Knock at the front door.

Now who's that? (*Alarmed.*) It'll be the Council. I knew they would.

From the back garden comes a sharp thwack, and then another. MARY *and* LILY *look out of the window. It is* HAROLD *with a battered putter, taking savage swings at the vegetation.* LILY *goes to answer the front door.*

HAROLD *comes for his jacket behind the door. He gestures upwards, trying to sort out something to say about* LEN, *but he can't.*

HAROLD. I'll tell you something, Mary: I may be only an ordinary puddler, but I'm not made of steel you know. I can only stand so much, I've as much feeling in me as anybody. I'd as lief get out of here to where I'm appreciated as not.

MARY. Ah now, Harold, you know you're happy here. And what about Lily?

HAROLD. Ah. Mmm. Yes. What *about* Lily. Isn't that just the point?

> HAROLD *goes out the back and then comes back.*

Have you seen his left hand? I mean, now that's not nice, is it?

> HAROLD *goes out again.* LILY *comes into the kitchen from the front, ushering* MRS MILNE. *She calls* MARY *into the kitchen.*

LILY. Mary! Mrs Milne, this is Mary. (*To* MARY.) It's Len's mother.

MRS MILNE. Pleased to meet you, Miss Thynne.

LILY. No, she's not my daughter. I like brought her up, from the Orphanage; she's always come to see me, even when she was little. We're very close.

MRS MILNE. Oh, that'll be nice for you, Miss Thynne. Have you none of your own?

LILY (*tiny pause*). No.

MRS MILNE. Is my Len in?

LILY. Now, that I don't know. He works nights, you see. And I'm off to work before he comes in mornings. Have you seen him, Mary?

MARY. No, but he *was* in.

MRS MILNE (*faintly*). Perhaps I might see him . . . Oh, all this talk. (*She sways.*)

MARY. Sit yourself down, missis.

MRS MILNE. Thank you.

LILY. There now, I bet she's worn out. Make her some tea,

Mary. (*To* MRS MILNE.) You'll have had a long trip. Where have you come from today, love?

MRS MILNE. Oh, all the way to Schofields' and then here.

LILY. Come by coach did you? Tiring.

MRS MILNE. Walking . . . walking . . .

LILY. Schofields'? Oh, you mean the shop.

MRS MILNE. I don't understand it. You tell me. What does he have to leave home for? Why does a man do a thing like that?

LILY. Oh. I thought he come from miles away.

MRS MILNE. It's a mile.

MARY. Of all the lying toads.

LILY. Now, Mary darling, you don't know.

MARY. Yes, I do; he distinctly said he'd been travelling.

LILY. Mary, you'll be so kind as to make a pot of tea before that blooming kettle is burnt right through to the handle!

MARY. Ooh, proud madam.

> MARY *flounces to the scullery.*

MRS MILNE. Now, I mustn't behave like this, must I? Whatever will you think? It's just that I'm worn out. I wanted to see how he was, you see, Mrs Thynne, and now I've seen you and I can rest easy. Bless you for looking after my boy. I should just like to see him for a minute if you'll be so kind as to call him, to give him these socks.

LILY. Yes, of course you would. I'll give him a call now. (*She goes to the hall.*) Mr Milne! Mr Milne! (*Coming back.*) I'm ever so sorry, Mrs Milne; he doesn't seem to be in.

> MRS MILNE *starts to go back out.* MARY *comes in from the scullery and makes for the hall.*

MRS MILNE. Oh, well, never mind. Will you give him these socks for me?

LILY (*taking them*). He's usually up by this time.

MARY (*goes upstairs*). It's no use just shouting. Shows how much you know about men.

MRS MILNE. No, never mind, dear.

MARY. His door's locked.

MRS MILNE. Locked!

LILY. That means he's out. You can't lock it from inside. Unless you bolt it.

MRS MILNE (*letting herself out*). Is this the way? Well, good-bye.

LILY. Good-bye, Mrs Milne. Call again.

We see MARY at the top of the stairs, the steps on the land-ing, and LEN's face peering down out of the attic trap-door. Fade out.

3. *A few days later. Midday. HAROLD is hunched miserably over the table in the kitchen, mopping up the remains of his dinner with a piece of bread. He has his overalls on. On the table by his plate there is a letter from the Council:*

Dear Sir,

   With reference to our letter of May 1st to which we have had no reply to date, and the visits of the Parks and Gardens officials on April 28th and May 4th, we have to inform you that the Borough Surveyor will call at your house on the afternoon of Wednesday, July 11 to discuss the height of your perimeter hedge with you.

   Your Obedient Servant,

SQUIGGLE

(Town Clerk).

We hear LILY's voice from the hall.

LILY (*off*). Len! Len!

   LEN *grunts in reply from his bedroom.*

There's some fresh tea and it's one o'clock!

   LEN *grunts from his room.* LILY *comes back into the kitchen from the hall wearing a pinafore. She pauses to take*

HAROLD's *plate. She looks absently at* HAROLD's *left hand.* HAROLD *becomes aware of this and straightens up self-consciously, hiding his left hand and toying with his teacup.* LILY *goes round to that side, sees that the cup is empty and takes it. She turns over a clean one ready for* LEN, *and goes out into the scullery.* HAROLD *grins ruefully to himself and goes for his jacket and cap.* LEN *comes into the kitchen, very frowsty, with his trousers pulled on over his pyjamas.*

LEN. Morning, Harold. You off back to work?

HAROLD. That's right. How're you getting on in your job?

LEN (*pouring himself tea*). What? Oh, same as usual . . . hard work and no overtime.

HAROLD. D'you get a bonus if you burn the works down?

LEN (*sly*). Oh . . . ah . . . you been asking questions.

HAROLD. Yes, I have, haven't I?

LEN. Yes, you have, haven't you (*Skilfully brushes crumbs off tablecloth with his left hand.*)

HAROLD. Mind, not that I'm saying there's anything wrong wi' being a stoker.

LEN. Well, o'course you an't, are you?

HAROLD. No, I haven't – don't.

> HAROLD *goes, discomfited.* LILY *comes in from the scullery and sits intimately with* LEN *at the table. He pours her some tea.*

LILY. First I've seen of you since Saturday, Len, when your mother came. Pity you missed her.

LEN. Ah.

LILY. What's this about you being a stoker? I thought you said engineer?

LEN. Well, it makes for a bit of interest, doesn't it? You mad at me?

LILY. Well, of course I am. Fibbing and fairy tales. What

d'you expect? And what about you cracking on you'd been
a wanderer, when all the time you'd been living with your
mum on this very self-same estate? It's just one thing on
top of another. How d'you think I must feel?

LEN. Honest, I didn't know you was bothered either way, so
I just made it as interesting as possible.

LILY. You think *I* wanted you to be a dirty old tramp?

LEN. I expect I thought you wanted a good idea to think about:
you know, taking a man desperate for accommodation. And
anyway, you could see I wasn't dirty. I smell a bit, I know,
but that's not from want of washing – that's natural.

LILY. You looked very nice to me, and I got used to . . .
(*Indicating his hand.*) And I like you altogether, hook line
and sinker, as you might say. (*Titters.*)

LEN. That's about the daftest thing I've heard you say.

LILY. That's not saying much, is it? You're never in to hear
me say anything.

LEN. Here, are you telling me you don't mind me being about
the place?

LILY. Yes.

LEN. Who, *me*?

LILY (*defensively*). You said all those lovely things first day.
You didn't have to ask then. I should have expected . . .
well . . . you'd take it for granted I'd be glad to see you.

LEN. Them wasn't lovely things; that was just true things what
I thought.

LILY. They made me happy.

LEN. Blimey, crikey, don't I feel humble now? And I am
enjoying this cup of tea, miss.

LILY. I'll make you some breakfast in a minute.

LEN. Oh, will you? Then I think I'll have a cigarette.

She goes to the mantelpiece for a light for him.

Now, here's something I can tell you about. (*He fishes a
box of twelve-bore cartridges out of his pocket.*) What d'you
think of that? They're cartridges for the gun.

LILY (*alarmed*). What gun?

LEN. Your dad's gun, o' course. I got it all cleaned up now, proper picture. I'll show you.

LILY. That you won't.

LEN. I had a look round in the attic, and you hadn't got none, and I thought: not much use, a gun, without bullets, so my mate got me some. There's a dozen there.

LILY. But great heavens, what's a gun for in the first place?

LEN. Well, you got it. I suppose you might as well have it. It's handy. You keep it around. In case.

LILY. In case of what?

LEN. Ah well, you never know till it's on you, do you? You get a pheasant nesting out there in the hedge, you shout to Harold, what's he going to do? You can't catch that class of a bird with a rolled-up newspaper.

LILY. Naturally not, when you've got a gun.

LEN. Ah. (*Sees letter on table.*) You got a letter, I see. That's nice.

LILY. Every time I get a letter now my heart stops. I bet it's from the Council, anyway. (*Reaches over for it.*) Yes, it is. You see? They're on about the perimeter again.

LEN. Now an't I told you? You're very foolish to be frightened. Everybody's frightened these days. I don't understand it. What you got to be frightened *about*? He won't eat you. I've yet to see a cannibal Borough Surveyor. What you got to lose?

LILY. You know very well what happens. These people, they keep talking and making you do things; they never stop, until you don't know who you are or where you are.

LEN. Look, Lily, if the Council makes you do something like you don't fancy, don't you do it because you're frightened?

LILY. Well, that's just what I say!

LEN. So if you ain't frightened in the first place you *don't have to touch that hedge.*

LILY. If I don't they will; they said so.

LEN. That's their look-out, innit? That's you making them do something.

LILY. Oh, is it heck.

LEN. It's them that's frightened, you mark my words. *You're* pushing *them* around in your own quiet way. I bet they're sweating cobs, that lot. And it's nothing to what they'll be when I finished, aha!

LILY. Don't be so stupid.

LEN. That's just what I am! Stupid! That's a big lump o' bone I got there. (*His head.*) Solid, right through to the middle. But you don't see me frightened, so now you tell me who's daft.

There is a knock at the front door.

LILY. That's the front door.

LEN. You stay here till I make reconnaissance. (*He goes out and then returns at once.*) You'll excuse me being so passionate with you just now. It's mostly affection, you know. I want to look after you and see things right for you, that's what it is.

LILY. I told you, it's nice having you here; I only hope you'll look after me the way I want to be looked after. You will, won't you?

LEN (*retreating*). Oh, I got my own way o' doing everything, an't I? (*He goes out to the hall.*)

LILY (*absently*). I had a feeling you might.

We see LEN at front door. He peeps out through the letter-box. Door knock. LEN comes smartly back to LILY in the kitchen.)

LEN. Right in one. Hairy old top-coat, shining brief-case, lot o' papers on a board and standing very close to the door. That's a borough surveyor O.K. (*Door knock.*) He'll have a big posh car waiting I shouldn't wonder, and another feller with him to do the measuring.

After a brief hesitation LILY *goes to open the front door.*
LEN *watches her go and then follows rapidly to behind her.*
Don't on no account let him in.

The BOROUGH SURVEYOR *is amazed to see this pyjamaed figure staring at him hostilely over* LILY's *shoulder.* LEN *scoots upstairs and then stops for a parting shot at the top of the stairs.*

This is the third time they been, Lily, and I an't let them in before. No liberties, Lily!

LEN *disappears along the landing and into his room.* LILY *turns, flustered, to the* SURVEYOR.

SURVEYOR. I seem to have chosen an unfortunate time. Please accept my apologies.

LILY. Oh, nothing like that . . .

SURVEYOR. Please . . . Miss Thynne? (*She nods.*) . . . What you do in your own house is no concern of mine. Er (*Consults his reports.*) . . . that was the gentleman who answered the door on the mornings of April 28th and May 4th, I imagine? Is he responsible (*Hastily.*) By that I mean is he your agent? Is he employed to act for you? Oh dear.

LILY (*terrified, shaking and blinking back tears*). He's nothing to do with me. He just lives here.

SURVEYOR. What I'm trying to get at, Miss Thynne, is about this hedge of yours.

LILY. His name's Milne. Mr Milne.

SURVEYOR. It's been extremely difficult for us, not being able to talk to you personally.

LILY. I work mornings.

SURVEYOR. Quite. Mr Milne . . . that's his name? Mr Milne seems to be in all day . . . and I can't have overtime on a matter like this. Well, you appreciate it's fortunate that you're in now. Mr. Milne's not very amenable, is he?

LILY. You could have come afternoons.

SURVEYOR. That's what we have done, now, isn't it?

LILY. Oh.

SURVEYOR. We don't want to bully you, but you must admit that it's rampant. The hedge. Now, it's rampant, isn't it? High and rampant.

LILY. Oh yes.

SURVEYOR. I've got a man here now who'll trim it for you, no bother, and, of course, no expense to you. (*Pause. He smiles.*) Perhaps if I could step inside for a second and we could discuss it. (*Old 'women are putty to me' coming it here.*) It's a small matter and all it wants is putting in perspective – won't take two ticks. (*Pause. More shortly.*) Now really, Miss Thynne, this whole business would be risible if it hadn't become so . . . protracted. Two official letters and several visits by Council workmen . . . it all costs money, you know.

There is a click from the road as the workman experiments with his shears. LEN *shouts indignantly from his bedroom window.*

LEN. Liberties! Don't think I don't see what you're up to there! By God!

WORKMAN (*in the road, very belligerent*). Oh, it's you is it, calf-head? (*He is suddenly alarmed.*) Get away with you with that thing! Mr Heginbottom!

SURVEYOR (*calling to the road*). Mr Heginbottom! Stop that carry-on, now! (*Looks up towards* LEN's *window.*) Heavens above, he's lost his wits. (*To* LILY.) He's pointing a gun at my man! Hey, hey, hey!

LILY *turns and runs up the stairs. We see the* WORKMAN *in the street, sidling towards the Council estate van which is parked just short of the gate.* MR HEGINBOTTOM *is in the driver's seat and very unhappy, twisting this way and that to see what's going on. The* WORKMAN *opens the back of the van, puts away the shears and takes out a short spade.*

He edges round the far side of the van towards the gate of the house.
We see LILY *banging frantically on* LEN's *door.*

LILY. Len! Don't do it, Len!

We see the WORKMAN *coming carefully and watchfully into the garden.*

WORKMAN. We'll see who's boss here. I've had a bellyful of his blether.

We see LILY *let into the bedroom by* LEN. *He clasps her comfortingly.*

LEN. They go too far, them fellers.

SURVEYOR (*shouting up the stairs*). Have you got a licence for that gun?

LEN (*going on to the landing*). This is a special gun; it don't need no licence to go bang, you just see.

LILY. Len! Len.

LEN *bangs the bedroom door closed on her and locks it. We see the* SURVEYOR *backing rapidly down the garden path. Shouts from the* WORKMAN.

WORKMAN. That'll do! That's enough!

LEN *comes down the stairs and steps out into the garden.*
We see LILY *in the bedroom rattling the door furiously, then she goes to the window and gazes fearfully down on to the emerging figure of* LEN.

The WORKMAN *steps from behind the retreating* SURVEYOR.
You'll put that gun down or else.

SURVEYOR (*from behind the van, to* LEN). This is nothing to do with you, sir!

LEN *carries the gun level in the crook of his arm. He advances. A step at a time. The* WORKMAN *stands his ground sturdily.*
LEN *comes to a halt a pace away from the* WORKMAN. *He*

leans over slightly to his right where there is a rotten-rusty piece of corrugated iron lining part of the path. He pushes his head forward in the aggressive-inquiring look of a cock-rooster. There is a harsh clang as he drives his hook across the level gun into the corrugated iron.

HEGINBOTTOM *starts the car. The* SURVEYOR *gets in. The* WORKMAN *spins round as he hears this and looks back at* LEN, *who has not moved.*

The van begins to move and the WORKMAN *legs after it, pulling open the back and leaping in.* LEN *watches it go and then returns to the house. He looks into the kitchen and then into the front room. Then he remembers and goes upstairs and unlocks the door of his room.*

LEN. There, see what I did? In my excitement I went and locked the door.

LILY (*eyes flashing*). I know what you did, you big ape!

LEN. Tell you what we'll do. Let's have a laugh on 'em, shall we? I'll cut the hedge down for you. There's a billhook in the shed, I seen it.

LILY. Ooh, you make me mad.

LEN. No, look, don't you see? They come back here all frantic for battle and full of blood-lust; and what do they see but you and me dancing about in the front garden for all the world to see and a two-foot hedge all round for pretty.

LILY. You're raving mad. You're stark raving mad.

LEN. Oh, I don't know, I soon shot them out, didn't I? I have these ideas, see.

LILY. Now you listen to me, Len Milne; you'll just let well alone, that's what you'll do, from now on.

LEN. Tell you what, I an't got it straight yet whether you want that hedge or not.

LILY. No, you haven't, have you? And it's none o' your business.

LEN. Well, don't be too sure. I don't suppose they'll be

delirious about me pointing that gun at them for a start. I had an argument with that feller with the spade before this.

LILY. You'd think at my time of life I shouldn't have to worry. I've worked hard, and I've kept myself nice. The house is mine and I haven't a penny debts, and *still* they won't leave me be. Why ? Because my hedge is higher ? Is that a reason ? No, I'm not asking you; you're no better than any of them. I don't know who sent you here to me, but I'll swear they meant me no good.

LEN. It was Mrs Schofield.

LILY. You'll have to go. There's no other answer for it; you'll have to take notice.

LEN. Oh. I slipped up somewhere along the line, I see. I an't going to inquire; no good'll come o' that. It was all meant for the best. You know that, don't you ? And I think the world of you. Oh, o' course I said that, didn't I ? Like, and I soon shot them off, didn't I ?

Both are finding this painful. LILY *can't speak for it.* LEN *wags his hook dispiritedly.*

It's handy though, innit ? See that feller with the spade jump sky-high when I banged the corrugated iron ? Not much I can't do with it. Of course, sometimes they give me a job that's a bit beyond me, like carrying, but I always find a way round. They had me with a wheelbarrow one time, bust my strap. So now I got an extra strong strap . . . goes round my shoulder. I expect I can take a week going ?

She takes hold of his left arm in both hands and kisses the hook.

Ah, I expect that's cool to you if your face is hot.

She sits on the bed, very upright, head hanging down, still holding his left hand. After a second he sits beside her. She raises her face. Without embracing her he kisses her very gently on the lips. Her hand flies to his shoulder as if to push him away and then rests there. She gives a murmuring

gurgling moan of pleasure, and he follows suit, a little self-consciously.
She draws away to look at him.

LILY. What's the matter?
LEN (*dizzy*). Matter? With me?
LILY. You just give a groan.
LEN. Oh, just for company, I suppose.

She kisses him briefly and then lowers her head to rest against him.

LILY. When I was a little girl . . .
LEN. Mm?
LILY. You mustn't be shamed by what I say. When I was a little girl . . . when I was twelve . . . I was alone in the house one time and my father came home and . . . and . . . what he did to me affected my whole life. (*Pause.*) Like he had relations with me, d'you see? (*Pause.*) I love him, d'you see? And our Mam, too. Well, that would be natural, wouldn't it? And I think he must have told . . . someone . . . confessed. So after that everything went cold and wrong, and I was took away and put with an auntie and then at a school . . . of course, I knew what it all meant, at the bottom of it, but everything went cold and wrong. And everybody was quiet, and distant. As if they were waiting for something to be over. That's why I've always looked after Mary, and asked for her to come from the Orphanage. There's no substitute for parents' love, is there? So anyway I was left . . . raw . . . I felt raw. You know, open.
LEN. That's bad. That's one of the worst things I ever heard.
LILY. You haven't heard much, have you?
LEN. No, it's usually me talking. I hope I'll know how to look after you right. I don't want you to come to no harm through me.
LILY (*smiling*). What are you talking about? I wasn't a

WAAF for nothing. I can look after myself, don't you worry.

LEN. Oh well, that's all right. What did you have to tell me what you just told me for ?

LILY. I wanted to tell you something.

LEN. Was it stories ?

LILY. No, but there's no law says you've got to believe it.

LEN. That's good, because I wouldn't know what to think of a thing like that.

LILY. Some people'd be glad to know and hold it against me; not everybody's like you.

LEN. Oh, they are mostly, I think.

We see MARY *coming into the scullery from outside. She looks round for* LILY.

MARY. Mother!

We see LEN *and* LILY *in the bedroom, lying back now, kissing but not embracing.* LILY's *hand flutters as before at his shoulder. We hear* MARY's *voice from downstairs.*

Moth-er!

We see MARY, *who is now at the foot of the stairs.*

Moth-er!

An upstairs door closes and LILY *comes sedately down the stairs.*

LILY. Oh, it's you, Mary, is it ? I was just making my bed.

MARY. You'd better watch you don't have to lie on it, hadn't you ?

LILY (*lightly as she passes* MARY). Whyever not, girlie ?

MARY (*following* LILY *into the kitchen*). For one thing, I'd like to know what all the fuss is about ?

LILY (*glowing*). Yes, people do make a fuss, don't they ? For something that's so soon over.

MARY (*firmly*). Who was it had the gun ?

LILY (*sobered a little*). Oh. Oh, that. (*Waves her hand vaguely.*) That was the lodger.

MARY. The lodger, the lodger? Last time I was here it was Len this and Len that. What's going on here?

LILY (*gaily*). I don't know *what* you're talking about.

MARY (*exasperated*). The estate's like a beehive all round. Cars coming and going. Guns out the bedroom window. Chasing the Council . . . I didn't know if I wasn't going to find you stretched out dead. The neighbours are all out looking.

LILY. Are they really? Oh.

MARY. Mother, you can't have that sort of thing.

LILY. The Council came bothering me about that hedge.

MARY. I know all that. You'll have to give him notice. What's people going to think?

LILY. Mary, he's a good kind man, I know he is. He acts strange at times . . .

MARY. Strange! He's eerie! Heaven knows what it looks like to the Council.

LILY. Blow the Council.

MARY. You can blow the Council if you like.

LILY. Oh, my God, daughter, you're all by yourself in the world and that's a fact.

MARY. Ah, there now, Mum, I didn't mean to be so sharp.

(*Goes to comfort her.*)

LILY. Now don't touch me. You're no better than anybody else. Getting at me and getting at me.

MARY *is stricken.*

No, no, forgive me, daughter. It's not me speaking. (*Holds* MARY's *hand.*) It's just that . . . I've come to love him, Mary, and you mustn't be jealous, because it's very wonderful. I know he's as daft as a brush, but you can't guess how he is with me.

MARY. You don't think you're going to be let, do you? It's

not over yet, you know. And what's our Harold going to
say to it ?

LILY. I know what I'm talking about, daughter. I've always
messed it up before. People, men have wanted me, really
wanted me. And I had all the love inside me, but I couldn't
get at it for them. (*She smiles.*) One fellow I always used to
call him by the wrong names. Broke his heart. You have to
smile. His name was Geoff . . . I think . . . or was it
Roger ? No, Geoff. And I used to call him anything but.

There is a knock at the back door. MARY *starts.*

MARY. There you are. I told you. The police already.

LILY (*looking and then going*). Get away. Can't you see it's
Mrs Gartside with a cup in her hand ?

LILY *opens the back door to* MRS GARTSIDE.

MRS GARTSIDE. Miss Thynne, have you such a thing as a
cup of sugar I could borrow till after ?

LILY. A funny thing, Mrs Gartside, I've run right out.

MRS GARTSIDE. There now. Hey, there's police car at your
front door, did you know ? *And* the Council. It'll be about
your lodger. Wan't it exciting, him chasing 'em off ? Good
on 'im, I say; they want showing.

MARY *goes to the front door.*

Stop 'em now love, else they'll have your front door what
colour they fancy and I don't know what-all, same as us
Council tenants.

We see MARY *opening the front door. The* BOROUGH
SURVEYOR *and the* POLICE SERGEANT *are a little taken
aback, because they haven't knocked yet.* MRS GARTSIDE
clacks on in the kitchen.

You know they made me take my leaded lights off, of course ?
They never *stop.*

MARY (*frightened and aggressive*). What d'you want ?

SURVEYOR. Is Miss Thynne in ?

MARY. No, she's not.

SURVEYOR (*with moderate patience*). Then who was that I heard talking just now?

MARY. One of the neighbours; she talks to herself. (*Shouts to kitchen.*) Shut up!

SURVEYOR (*quietly to the* POLICE SERGEANT). I tell you, the whole house is raving.

POLICE SERGEANT. We'd like to speak to the man who owns the gun, please.

SURVEYOR. Mr Milne's his name, I believe.

> MARY *turns and goes upstairs. Silence.* MRS GARTSIDE *peers out of the kitchen door and dodges back again. So does* LILY. *On the landing we see* MARY *try* LEN's *bedroom door, it is locked. There is a chair out on the landing.* MARY *comes back down to the front door. We see* LEN *peering out of the trap-door to the attic.*

MARY. He's not in.

SURVEYOR. I'll tell you what our problem is. It's that hedge. Now, anyone can see it's rampant. Leaving aside that it defies a bylaw, it constitutes a nuisance to passers-by, and . . . I don't mean to be offensive . . . *and* I should guess it's a bit of an eyesore to you living here.

MARY. I don't live here.

SURVEYOR. What we were hoping was that we could be allowed to trim it for you . . . quite free of charge.

MARY. Oh well, if you put it like that . . .

SURVEYOR. We could apply for a court order . . . but that's not a way to do things, now is it?

MARY. A court order? Has he given someone a baby?

SURVEYOR. What I mean to say is, while the law *is* on our side we want to ask your permission to tidy it up quickly and quietly.

MARY. All right, then. It's nowt to me, but it seems all right. Only I should be sharp about it.

SURVEYOR. Thank you. I must say it's a pleasure to talk to someone sensible.

MARY. That's what I meant about being sharp.

The BOROUGH SURVEYOR's *beaming smile fades slightly. He and the* POLICE SERGEANT *retire.* MARY *closes the door and goes back to the kitchen.*

Outside in the road we see the POLICE SERGEANT *taking his leave of* HEGINBOTTOM *and the* BOROUGH SURVEYOR, *who are in their van, and going back to the police car. The* WORKMAN *is getting out his clippers and a billhook. On the landing we see* LEN *lowering himself out of the attic on to the chair. In the kitchen the three women stand in a group, tensely listening.*

Click go the clippers experimentally. Then click, click.

We see LEN, *outraged, wrenching open his bedroom door and hurtling in.*

Down in the kitchen the women are listening in suspense to the sound of LEN's *movements above as he re-emerges from his bedroom, slams the doors and thunders downstairs . . . missing several at the bottom with a clatter and a crash. We get a glimpse of him from the hall as he throws open the front door crash against the wall and dashes into the garden, shotgun in hand, and we hear two evenly spaced and very loud bangs. We see* MRS GARTSIDE's *face as she screams as loud as she can, in a series of bursts,* LILY *and* MARY *staring at her blankly.*

LEN *in the garden among the weeds, the gun held high and vertical and the gunsmoke above him. The police car turning in the road to come back.*

The Council estate van has started and pulls away; pursued by the WORKMAN, *who pulls open the back and scrambles in. In the garden* LEN *puts the gun between his knees to break it, takes out the cases and reloads.* MRS GARTSIDE's *screams subside.*

The heat of the gun barrel finally scorches LEN's *knees and he drops it. Picks it up again, raises it high and vertical and fires both barrels again.*
Redoubled screams from MRS GARTSIDE.

4. *The Police Station: Daytime: Studio.*

The BOROUGH SURVEYOR *rushes in and goes to the duty* POLICEMAN *at the desk.*

SURVEYOR. You must send armed men at once to the Farm, in Mather Road. Armed!

The POLICEMAN *jumps up and then sits down again. He takes out a notepad and looks at the* SURVEYOR *cheerfully.*

POLICEMAN. You gave me quite a little start there, sir. What is it? Your one-armed bandit again?

SURVEYOR. He's a maniac. He's firing off that shotgun in every conceivable direction.

POLICEMAN. Well, we all have our little ways, don't we, sir? There's a squad car there at this very moment, so you take it easy. They'll sort it out. There's been no complaint as such so far.

SURVEYOR. No complaint? Do I have to have little holes in my head before I'm allowed the liberty of complaining. What am I doing now if I'm not complaining?

POLICEMAN (*soothing*). Nothing, sir, but who knows, you could very easily have been trespassing, for instance.

SURVEYOR. I'll for instance you. Where's the sergeant? Complaint.

POLICEMAN. The sergeant's in the squad car, isn't he? Didn't he go off with you?

SURVEYOR. Oh yes, so he did.

The squad car draws up outside.

POLICEMAN. Ah, that'll be him.

> *The driver of the squad car comes in with* LEN, *still carrying the gun, followed by the* SERGEANT.

SURVEYOR. Take that gun off him!

POLICEMAN (*quietly to the* SERGEANT *re the* SURVEYOR). He's very excited, Serge.

SERGEANT (*to* LEN). I think you can relinquish that gun for a few moments now, Mr Milne. It's very kind of you to come along.

> LEN *props the gun against the counter.*

LEN. It wants a bit of sorting out, don't it?

SURVEYOR. Oh, for goodness' sake impound the weapon. For one thing, I'm convinced he hasn't got a licence.

LEN. It's not my gun, if that's what you think.

SURVEYOR. Whose is it?

LEN. Harold Thynne's father's.

SURVEYOR. And where's he?

LEN. How should I know? He's dead.

SURVEYOR. Dead? How?

LEN. Now, that I couldn't tell you. Might have been sudden shock or perhaps pneumonia . . . all I know is it was a good few years ago.

SURVEYOR. It's quite clear he hasn't got a licence, Sergeant. Take it off him; he's dangerous.

SERGEANT. Now now, sir, he doesn't need a licence for that.

SURVEYOR. He doesn't? So he can blaze away, point-blank, at anyone he pleases?

SERGEANT. How far away were you, sir, when he fired?

SURVEYOR. A matter of feet, both Heginbottom and myself. But it's not myself I'm concerned for. One of my men . . . he's outside now in the van . . . was less than *three feet away*.

SERGEANT. Anybody hit? Or any damage?

SURVEYOR. No!

SERGEANT. Not a very good shot, is he, sir? Now, Mr Milne, you fired off that shotgun?

LEN. That's just what I did, sergeant, four bullets; and they run off like billy-o. Did you see them?

SERGEANT. Now, don't you think that's just a teeny bit dangerous?

LEN. Oh yes. But I fired in the air. I reckoned that was safest.

SERGEANT. Quite right, it *is* the safest, if you're going to fire at all. But still, it might lead to a breach of the peace.

LEN. Or a breach of the Borough Surveyor, eh, Sergeant?

SERGEANT. I hope not, Mr Milne.

LEN. So do I, Sergeant, you may take my oath.

SERGEANT. . . . and it *is* risky, now isn't it?

LEN. Extremely risky.

SERGEANT. That's just what I say, extremely risky. (*Pause.*)

LEN. Risky.

SERGEANT. Well, think on what I've said, won't you Mr Milne? Good afternoon.

LEN. Good afternoon. Good afternoon, all. Excuse me.

> LEN *picks up the gun and starts to go. He stops, and with the flicker of a glance at the* BOROUGH SURVEYOR *addresses the* SERGEANT.

Extremely risky . . .

SERGEANT. . . . and might lead to a breach of the peace. Yes.

> LEN *goes.*

5. *The Farm: Daytime: Studio.*

> *Milk bottles on the step, one with a note in it. Windows all closed. Round the back the clothes line is clear. Everything very still. Bare hallstand except for* LEN's *cap and coat. In the front room,* LILY *in her outdoor clothes. Two cases by her.*
> MARY *comes in at the front door and into the front room.*

MARY. I've got one. He'll be here in a few minutes.

LILY. I could just as well have walked.

MARY. Now, don't be silly, Mother, not with a bag and two cases and all. And anyway what's the rush? You're not running away. You're going to have a rest and a holiday from here.

LILY (*suddenly*). I *can't* stay, can I, Mary? There's . . . people all over the place and I can't think straight. I've got to go away if only to think straight. Wouldn't it be nice if there was only one thing you wanted . . . just joining with a man.

MARY. Now, don't start up again.

LILY. Well, how would *you* feel? Isn't it only natural to want to feel added to? To feel that you win something when you go courting with a man?

MARY. Ouf! Me courting! That's a good 'un.

LILY. Don't you be surprised, I know he's unselfish and good, and he never thinks of himself.

MARY. Some hopes.

LILY. Oh, it's true, Mary, he's got a beautiful nature if you did but know. It's not fair. He's a hundred good things that many a woman's man isn't, but he's not a husband. I couldn't look after him or be looked after like any ordinary housewife, could I? If I had a time-bomb in the house it'd be easier, because the neighbours wouldn't have to know. I'm only ordinary, Mary, and he just doesn't care . . . he'd take on the world and not even care who wins.

MARY. Pull yourself together, Mother. You said yourself you're going away to *think*.

LILY. That's just stories between you and me, Mary. He wouldn't do a thing like this. (*Bitterly*.) 'Careless Rapture.' The people that write them books just don't know, do they? D'you think they'll arrest him after what he's done?

MARY. If you ask me he should have been arrested before. He's a menace. Anyway, you've finished with him now.

The front door opens and closes as LEN *comes back in. He still has the shotgun.*

MARY *gives* LILY *a warning look.* LEN *goes to the kitchen. Finding no one there, he returns to the hall.* MARY *opens the front-room door a crack to spy if it's* LEN *or* HAROLD. LEN *looks at her through the crack.*

LEN. Is Lily in?

MARY (*opens the door wider, but not moving out of the way*). Yes.

LEN (*calls*). Hallo, Lily. I settled that, then.

MARY *steps aside and* LEN *goes into the room. He looks at* LILY *and her luggage.*

Oh. You off, then?

LILY. I'm going away for a bit.

LEN. Hope you have a nice time. I'll look after the place, don't you worry, Lily. How long you going for?

LILY. Just a few days.

MARY. Mother, the taxi's here.

MARY *goes to the front door, taking the cases.* LILY *stands up.*

LEN. I'm sorry you're going just now.

LILY. Oooh, Len, so am I. I don't want to go away. (*She cries helplessly, looking straight at him, careless of her appearance.*) Aren't you going to try and stop me?

LEN. Well, I don't know how to set about it. I mean, you made arrangements. Did you promise?

LILY *nods.*

I'll be lonely. But it'll be all right when you come back.

MARY (*off*). Mother!

LILY. I don't want to go away.

LEN. Now, you're not to worry. Everything'll be all right.

LILY. Good-bye, Len.

LEN. So long, Lily. Keep well.

He stands aside and she goes out. He follows, watching her go. The taxi leaves. LEN *puts the gun in the hallstand and goes upstairs.* MARY *would like to get a quick decision, but she hesitates and* LEN *is nearly at his room before she speaks.*

MARY. Where are you going to go, then?

LEN (*off*). Oh, I'll just have a lie down, I think.

MARY. No, I mean . . . for digs? There's plenty of cards in Schofield's window. Are you there? Where are you?

LEN *comes back to the top of the stairs.*

LEN. It seems to me you got it all wrong.

MARY. Now, don't you get funny with me.

LEN. I don't get funny with nobody; it's you. You took against me first time you saw me, so everything I do is wrong. Lily gave me notice, I know that, and so do you seemingly, but she didn't mean it. So you just get her here before you start making accusations.

MARY. She's not coming back here until you've gone. That was the arrangement.

LEN. A lot you know. I only just this minute sorted out the Council on her behalf.

MARY. You've got a cheek bringing that up! I suppose that's your idea of finished? They'll be back, of course they will. Racketing around, that's the whole point. How d'you think Lily feels?

LEN. Oh.

MARY. Well, you soppy thing, d'you think she wants people firing guns?

LEN. Thank you very much, Mary; I hadn't thought of that. I won't do it again.

MARY (*impatient*). Oooh! D'you want a cup of tea?

LEN (*comes downstairs*). I'll make you one, shall I?

MARY. But mark what I say: you'll have to leave.

LEN (*going into the kitchen*). Oh, you got it all wrong.

MARY *stamps her foot with impatience.*

Fade out.

6. *Evening: a week later.*

MRS MILNE *approaches the front door and knocks. In the kitchen* HAROLD *is having his tea and reading the paper. He gets up to answer the door with a butty in his hand. He shows her into the kitchen.*

LEN *comes out of his bedroom with his trousers on over his pyjamas as usual. He quietly opens the front door and creeps across the garden to the hedge and peers close. On the other side* MRS GARTSIDE *and a* NEIGHBOUR *are startled to see him so close and so suddenly. They walk stiffly and briskly away.* LEN *watches the neighbours until they've gone and then returns to the house.*

At the bottom of the stairs HAROLD *is about to call upstairs for* LEN *as he walks quietly in.* HAROLD's *voice comes out muffled with food.*

HAROLD. Len!

The sudden shout startles LEN *into shutting the door more loudly than he intended.* HAROLD *spins round in alarm and chokes on his food. He sits on the stairs and gestures wildly for assistance.* LEN *pounds his back.*

MRS MILNE *and* MARY *come bustling out of the kitchen and drag them apart.*

MARY. Honestly, men, you can't leave 'em alone together for two minutes.

MRS MILNE (*levelling a hatpin aggressively at* HAROLD). Go straight into the kitchen, Len.

LEN. Hello, Mam.

LEN *goes into the kitchen, followed by* MARY.

MARY. Come on, the pair of you, where I can keep my eye on you. Len, your mother's come for you. You won't believe me; perhaps you'll believe her.

MRS MILNE (*to* HAROLD). Great big fellow like you . . . go on, you can go in now.

HAROLD *goes into the kitchen, followed by* MRS MILNE.

LEN. I don't know about you, Harold, but I've had about enough of this for the time being.

HAROLD. I've had about enough of everything.

LEN. Let's go out for a walk.

MARY. Just hold on!

LEN. Ah, now leave off, Mary, there's a good girl. You got it all wrong.

MARY. You've been saying that all week, ever since Lily left. You tell him, Mrs Milne.

MRS MILNE. Lenny boy, this young lady came to look me out. I know all about what happened.

LEN. Well, it was all a misunderstanding. It won't happen again.

MRS MILNE. I mean about Miss Thynne.

LEN. That's right. Only trouble is I went a bit far, and now the Council's too frightened to come near. Still, it established a principle, dinnit? Even if nobody wanted it establishing. Perhaps they'll come again. If they don't I'll have a go at trimming it. Don't you worry, Mary. I see you got a letter. That's nice.

MARY *looks at the letter on the mantelpiece.*

MARY. It's for you.

LEN. Don't be silly; only my mam knows I'm here, and she's here.

MARY *hands him the letter.*

MRS MILNE. It's about Miss Thynne, Len; she doesn't want you here, darling.

LEN. She's not here herself, so how can it bother her?

MARY (*to* MRS MILNE). You see what I mean? He's like this all the time; you can't get sense out of him.

LEN. I don't think there's any malice in Mary, Mam, only she don't understand, see. Such love as I bear Lily Thynne . . . such love as I bear . . . it wouldn't make sense, nothing would make sense if . . . if . . . Ask Harold, ask anybody, ask Lily when she comes back: I didn't *want*, don't *want* anything of her, see? Oh blimey, crikey, it's a very difficult subject to *approach*, this is. But look, I know I made a racket a couple of times . . . well, that's just me, innit? You know that, Mam. But I keep to my room, and I go in and out, ask Harold; and I wouldn't do nor say anything that I thought was out of place and not acceptable to . . . to Lily. (LEN *opens the letter*.) I expect somebody's made a mistake . . . oh no. (*Reads*.) 'Dearest Len.' Must be from a woman. (*Reads*.)

MRS MILNE. Len, Len dearest, Mary's taken me to the store where Miss Thynne works. She's still there, at the cash desk. She's not been away. She's been there all the time. She's just not been here; this is the only place she hasn't been.

LEN (*looks up blankly from the letter*). She's not been away; she's just not been here?

He gets up and goes out of the back door. They watch. He goes to a shed and re-emerges with a billhook. He moves round the house out of sight. HAROLD *follows him out a little way and then stops.* MARY *picks up the letter. In the road outside at the front the Council estate van is parked just before the hedge. In it: The* BOROUGH SURVEYOR, MR HEGINBOTTOM *and a different* WORKMAN.

SURVEYOR. This is the place. We'll stand by till you get

started, and then come back later to see how you've got on and drive you home.

2ND WORKMAN. This is The Farm, isn't it? I thought you told me it wasn't the place where Harry Smethurst and you got chased off with a shotgun?

SURVEYOR. You've nothing to worry about. He works nights. For goodness' sake, why d'you think you're coming here at a time like this? On time and a half?

2ND WORKMAN. But he got shot at!

SURVEYOR. The shots were fired in the air.

2ND WORKMAN. I knew there was something fishy.

SURVEYOR. Fishy?

2ND WORKMAN. I know what you're up to. Well, nobody makes a clay pigeon out of me.

SURVEYOR. This job will bring down my grey hairs to the grave. Look, what's your name?

2ND WORKMAN. Never you mind my name!

SURVEYOR. I give you my word of honour you'll come to no harm.

2ND WORKMAN. All right then, you do it.

SURVEYOR. Don't be ridiculous, I wouldn't know how to begin.

2ND WORKMAN. Borough Surveyor and he doesn't know how to cut a hedge, marvellous.

SURVEYOR (*swallowing*). Very well, I'll tell you what I'll do: I'll stand out there with you. Will that satisfy you?

The WORKMAN *gets suspiciously out of the van after the* SURVEYOR. *After a moment the* WORKMAN *begins to cut with the billhook. He slashes heavily and goes through a branch cleanly. He drags it away and is about to cut again when we hear* LEN's *billhook thud into the hedge just round the corner inside the garden. The* WORKMAN *pauses and then goes to the gate to look through and across the corner. The* SURVEYOR *follows.*

2ND WORKMAN. Hey! What d'you think you're on! This is my job!

LEN. I was just cutting it down 'fore I go.

2ND WORKMAN. Well, you needn't bother!

LEN. It's one thing I got to do.

> *The* WORKMAN *takes an indignant step forward and then has a thought. He looks round for the* SURVEYOR, *who is rapidly gaining the van.*

2ND WORKMAN. The Maniac with the Hook. That treacherous bastard, he'd have left me to his mercy.

> *He gazes, fascinated, at* LEN. *He is joined by* MRS GARTSIDE *and the* NEIGHBOUR, *and makes a place for them to watch.* HAROLD *comes round the corner of the house and stops a few paces from* LEN. MARY *and* MRS MILNE *come round past* HAROLD, MARY *still holding the letter. By now* LEN *has cut on, glass-eyed, desperately, steadily.*

MRS MILNE. Lenny boy, it's getting late. Isn't it time you was at work?

MARY. You don't have to do that, you know.

LEN (*not stopping*). I an't coming back to live with you, you know, Mam.

MRS MILNE. No, Len, I understand: you want to live your own life.

LEN. Well, I wouldn't be too sure about that . . . me wanting to live my own life, not judging by the dose I had so far. But I got to live it, an't I?

> *The* WORKMAN *has come round outside to the gap and now looks cautiously through.*

WORKMAN. I'll give you a hand if you like.

> LEN *stops to look at him, billhook poised, then carries on.*

LEN. I got a hand.

MRS GARTSIDE *and the* NEIGHBOUR *have come to the gap, and* HEGINBOTTOM *and the* BOROUGH SURVEYOR *approach.*

2ND WORKMAN. What's up?

LEN *takes the letter from* MARY's *hand and hands it to the* WORKMAN. *We see it as the* WORKMAN *reads it:*

Dearest Len,

I should like to give you notice from last Saturday.

Yours sincerely,

Lily Thynne.

Well, that's not the end of the world, is it?

LEN. I haven't noticed. D'you know there are some times when you wish you were just nothing? One time I asked my little nephew I said: 'What d'you want to be when you grow up? Here's a penny.' 'A man,' he says, 'and I want sixpence.' I had to laugh. Not a bad ambition either, is it? I'll tell you something, that's the finish of me in this house.

LEN *goes back to his hacking, gradually leaving the little group behind.*

Introduction to

THE KITCHEN—*Arnold Wesker*

Audrey Coldron

THE PLAYWRIGHT AND HIS WORK

Though not his first play to be presented on the stage, *The Kitchen* was the first play Wesker wrote. In all his early plays he makes great use of autobiographical material. He had worked in a kitchen both as a porter and as a pastrycook, and he draws directly on these experiences in this play. Later, in his trilogy— a series of three inter-related plays: *Chicken Soup with Barley*, *Roots* and *I'm Talking About Jerusalem*—he reflects his early life in a London, East-end, Jewish family; and the character of the son, Ronnie (a poet, a disillusioned communist and ardent socialist who works in London, Norwich and Paris as a pastry-cook) is essentially Wesker himself. In *Chips With Everything* he writes of his National Service in the R.A.F.

He refers to himself as being 'theatrically uneducated' when he wrote *The Kitchen* and the trilogy. It wasn't until he went to the London School of Film Technique that he received encouragement in his writing. This probably accounts for the boldness of his attempts and his having managed in some of his seven plays to avoid the traditional three-act strait-jacket and to develop instead, forms more suited to his themes and subjects. He undoubtedly owes much of his flexibility to his film training.

Wesker is one of the dramatists once referred to as 'kitchen-sink writers' and in his early plays he tries to present natural-istically the conversations of working-class people.

He is what might be called a committed writer, expressing without apology or ambiguity his socialist ideas. This does not mean his plays are merely political tracts—socialist theories spouted forth by puppets. Believing that in a capitalist society man is frustrated or exploited, he presents situations in which human beings are seen to be at the mercy of social forces and their agents. In some cases the characters fight against them, as do the communist Kahns in *Chicken Soup* and the Simmonds in *I'm Talking About Jerusalem*. But the failure to achieve 'a New Jerusalem in England's green and pleasant land' is seen to be not a failure of socialism but the result of human weaknesses and the power of the capitalist machine.

Wesker, however, is generally considered to be an optimistic writer; even in relentless conditions there is humour, humanity—often hope. One of his major concerns is popular culture—this is expressed most clearly in *Roots*, the second play of the trilogy, considered by many people to be his best play to date.

In 1960 Wesker made public his idea for a project that takes another step towards bringing about practical opportunities for popular culture. That September the T.U.C. Resolution Number 42 had called on the Trades Union Movement to examine the need to participate more fully in the Arts, so Wesker conceived the idea of Centre 42 which he hoped would be supported in every way by the Trade Unions. In 1961 and 1962, Arts Festivals were mounted in a number of cities at the invitation of Trade Councils, but Wesker saw the need for a permanent centre. In July 1964 Wesker acquired the Roundhouse in Chalk Farm, London to be the permanent home of Centre 42 but the project was dogged by commercial penury and the Centre 42 Trust was finally wound up in 1970.

Chicken Soup with Barley was his first play to be staged—by the Belgrade Theatre, Coventry in 1958 and later the same year at the Royal Court Theatre, London. *Roots* followed at both theatres in 1959 and *I'm Talking About Jerusalem* in 1960. The 'Court' staged the complete trilogy later the same year. By this time *The Kitchen* had been staged (in 1959). *Chips With Everything* was produced in 1962, *The Four Seasons* in 1965, a play with a significantly Weskerian title *Their Very Own and*

Golden City in 1966 and *The Friends* in 1970, ironically enough at the Round House in Chalk Farm.

It may be useful to read the play at this point before continuing with the introduction.

THEME AND CHARACTERS

Some plays tell a story, others explore characters, themes or a situation. *The Kitchen* centres round a day's activity in the kitchen of a large and busy restaurant that serves two thousand lunches every day. This kitchen is a relentless machine of which the workers seem to become a part. A number of people come to work in it and as we observe and listen to them, we begin to realize how far their lives are affected by their working conditions. Lunch time approaches and the system gathers speed; the workers are forced along with it, unable to opt out—able only to accept or to complain.

The play is in fact about industrial society and its effects on all involved in it. Wesker sees the kitchen not only as a force in itself but also as an image. He puts the explicit statement first into the mouth of Dimitri, the sensitive Cypriot porter—'[This stinking kitchen is like the world—you know what I mean ?*]... Why you grumble about this one kitchen ?' (p. 121). And a little later Peter says, 'You and the kitchen. And the kitchen don't mean nothing to you and you don't mean to the kitchen nothing. Dimitri is right you know—why do you grumble about this kitchen ? [The world is filled with kitchens—only some they call offices and some they call factories*]' (p. 122).

The kitchen is a clearly-defined, naturalistic setting for a variety of human relationships and of conflicts—in work, of race, of temperament and emotion. It provides a study of different attitudes—to work, to coping with pressures, to provocation, to money and to friendship. In charge is Mr. Marango, the boss who is machine-like in his responses and in

* From the original and shorter version of *The Kitchen* 1960 Penguin Books.

his lack of understanding of his workers' needs beyond their basic material ones. Why is the environment so relentless? How much is this related to the size of the restaurant? Kevin says, 'Even in the small restaurants they're not after caring much' (p. 108).

Wesker also suggests through his play some of the effects of the industrial machine. For example Dimitri's comment, '... in a factory a man makes a little piece till he becomes a little piece' (p. 89). And the Chef's rejection of the suggestion that work is to be enjoyed. It is a means of keeping up a standard of living (p. 105). And Peter in response to a remark that the job at the Tivoli is bad says, '... what is there a man can't get used to? Nothing! You just forget where you are and you say it's a job' (p. 106).

Wesker speaks of Peter after three years in this same kitchen as 'living on his nerves', and he sees the noise and activity of the kitchen as generating a kind of frenzy. Notice how often he uses words and phrases associated with madness. And there is always the possibility of violence. Amidst the constant heat from the ovens, the noise they make which builds to a roar, in the steam and the sweat, among the tools and the knives, the human conflicts and aspirations can find no outlet. Bickerings, tormentings, prejudices and frustrations accompany the threat of violence which runs through the play. There are references again and again to Peter's fight with Gaston, there are many threats and quarrels, there is the scalding of Hans and finally Peter's last wild outburst in which frenzy issues into physical action.

So the socialist Wesker depicts the industrial machine as robbing a man of dignity in a soul-destroying job, simply for money. In the third play of his trilogy *I'm Talking About Jerusalem* he examines this same theme in a different way. He makes one character speak of 'an old truth: that a man is made to work and that when he works he is giving away something of himself, something precious,' and he himself quotes William Morris as saying, 'Machines are all right to relieve dull and dreary work, but man must not become a slave to them'.

The effect of the machine is highlighted in the scene of the afternoon lull when the ovens are low and the men speak of their dreams. (Cf. Hans' earlier dream of going to America—a dream of superfluity and high-living.) Each dream indicates ways in which society is not supplying human needs. Though Peter cannot express a dream perhaps there is a hint at the beginning of the scene of the kind of dream he might have supplied. In the rush hour it is every man for himself (cf. p. 118). Before the rush, or here in the quietness of the afternoon, there can be discussion, an attempt to listen, to communicate and understand, but one wonders how far the characters succeed in revealing themselves and communicating with the others in that scene?

The Kitchen is of unusual construction. There are numerous speaking parts and during most of the play many people are busily engaged on the stage; the action is carried forward in snatches of dialogue, conversation and activity, woven together in an intricate pattern as they emerge from the humming or roaring background, which take the attention of the audience and then sink back.

The main character is Peter, not simply because Wesker gives him most to do, but because he epitomises the problems and effects of this world of the kitchen. This particular day in the life of the kitchen is his day. It is the day when his frustrations and frenzies reach eruption point and his outbreak brings the whole world to a halt, draws a human cry from the chef and a question from Mr. Marango that urgently needs an answer.

Peter is German—automatically to be regarded with suspicion by some as a 'Boche'. He appears, especially in early conversation with Kevin, to have adjusted to the conditions. He is generally good-humoured but his pranks are childish and his laughter verges on the hysterical. We are told quite early on that he usually grows more and more quarrelsome as the day goes on—'I say good morning to Peter but never good night'

(p. 87). And the suspicion that the adjustment is superficial is confirmed when the relationship with Monique finally cracks and he breaks out in the violent attack on the kitchen. His attitude has never been one of acceptance, however, though his defiance has been covert—face-pulling behind the back of authority, mutterings under the breath. The scene with the tramp indicates his basic humanity and lack of conformity with authority.

There is no development of characters and relationships. They are revealed in the course of dialogue and action as we see how they respond to or cope with the environment. Apart from Peter the parts are not large but they are lively, convincing characters, well-contrasted, each weaving a distinctive thread in the total pattern. Kevin as the new cook serves usefully to respond as a newcomer to the environment, to register protest and to provoke comment. Dimitri the Cypriot kitchen porter is the only one who seems to be able to face up to and accept his situation; he is perceptive about his work and his fellow-workers; he finds fulfilment in his hobby, his dream being of a workshop where he could develop his interest. He is making the best of a bad job, and he serves to point up the discontent, insecurity and unhappiness of the others.

It is generally a weakness in an author if his dialogue and actions so insufficiently reveal his characters that he must write notes about them. But perhaps Wesker's notes show only a young writer's lack of confidence in his ability to communicate his characters in the text, or he may simply be nervous about the ability of his actors to glean the material for themselves.

ACTING AND PRODUCTION

All acting must be teamwork, each actor giving what is needed to the total play and responding suitably to the other actors. But this play in particular needs sensitive co-operation between actors and between actors and producer. One can think of it as being like a piece of orchestral music. Most of the instruments are playing together but at any given moment one or two are playing the main tune and all the others are providing a suitable accompaniment. As other instruments take the tune, the previous ones merge into the background harmony. The players need to concentrate all the time, to be sensitive to the total effect and obey the conductor's instructions.

This is a naturalistic play and should convince the audience of its authenticity. Wesker, to help the players achieve this, supplies detailed advice which should be looked at carefully and each member of the cast must work hard to portray his character as efficient at his particular job in the kitchen. The professional cast who first presented the play learned how to do their jobs with real food in real kitchens so that they could be convincing when miming food on the stage. It is worth trying, as far as possible, to practise with real food and observe real cooks in action, so that each actor can carry out his job in mime, convincingly, at top speed, during the rush hour.

The action must not be a series of short jerky scenes. Except in the 'lull' sequence and at the very end, the activity is continuous; the kitchen is a hive of industry. The producer must see that there is suitable activity but that it is never distracting, that nothing other than basic kitchen business is carried on as accompaniment. On the other hand the scenes and dialogues do not arise from a vacuum. Wesker sometimes indicates the lead up to the scene, for instance. While Kevin has been introduced and is talking to the pastrycooks, Bertha has entered. This must be timed so that she has completed her business and Nicholas entered by Paul's final line, so that Nicholas can bring out his first words and the dialogue is carried forward.

Timing and pace are important. There should be variety between scene and scene, avoiding an even pace; the general tempo should increase through Part I up to the Interlude accelerating at the end, then slackening during the lull. Part II follows a similar but less extreme pattern, the 'lull' at the end being completely different in mood and intensity.

The Kitchen

ARNOLD WESKER

INTRODUCTION
AND NOTES FOR THE PRODUCER

The lengthy explanations I am forced to make may be annoying; I am sorry, but they are necessary.

This is a play about a large kitchen in a restaurant called the Tivoli. All kitchens, especially during service, go insane. There is the rush, there are the petty quarrels, grumbles, false prides, and snobbery. Kitchen staff instinctively hate dining-room staff, and all of them hate the customer. He is the personal enemy. The world might have been a stage for Shakespeare but to me it is a kitchen, where people come and go and cannot stay long enough to understand each other, and friendships, loves and enmities are forgotten as quickly as they are made.

The quality of the food here is not so important as the speed with which it is served. Each person has his own particular job. We glance in upon him, highlighting as it were the individual. But though we may watch just one or a group of people, the rest of the kitchen staff does not. They work on.

So, because activity must continue while the main action is played out, we shall study, together with a diagram of the kitchen, who comes in and what they do.

The waitresses spend the morning working in the dining-room before they eat their lunch. But throughout the morning there are about three or four who wander in and out carrying glasses from the glassery to the dining-room and performing duties which are mentioned in the course of the play. During the service the waitresses are continually coming out of the dining-room and ordering dishes from the cooks. The dishes are served on silver and the waitresses take about six plates out of the hot-plate immediately under the serving-counter. Stocks of plates are replenished all the time by the porters. These are highly efficient waitresses. They make a circuit round the kitchen calling at the stations they require. They move fast and carry large quantities of dishes in their arms.

The kitchen porters, who are a mixture of Cypriots and Maltese, are divided into various sections. Firstly there are those who do the actual washing of cutlery, tins and plates by machine; these we do not see. For our purpose we only use one porter, who continually replaces clean plates under the serving-counter so that the waitresses can take them as required. He also sweeps up at regular intervals and throws sawdust around.

The woman who serves the cheeses and desserts and coffee, we hardly and rarely see through the glass partition back of stage, but every now and then she comes to the pastry-section to replenish her supplies of tarts and pastries.

Now to the cooks. At this point it must be understood that at no time is food ever used. To cook and serve food is of course just not practical. Therefore the waitresses will carry empty dishes, and the cooks will mime their cooking. Cooks being the main characters in this play, I shall sketch them and their activity here, so that while the main action of the play is continuing they shall always have something to do.

NOTE

The section dealing with the service starting on p. 111 with 'Two veal cutlets' is the actual production worked out by John Dexter based on what was originally only an indicative framework set out by me. I wish to acknowledge his creation of this workable pattern.

The pattern of service falls into three stages of increasing speed. (1) From 'Two veal cutlets,' p. 111, to Gaston's 'Max send up steaks and mutton chops quick,' p. 114, the pace is brisk but slow. (2) From then on to Peter's cry of 'Too old, too old my sweetheart,' p. 116, the pace increases. (3) From then on to the end of the part, 'Have you all gone barking-raving-bloody-mad,' the pace is fast and hectic.

If trouble is taken to work out this pattern then the right rhythm will be found.

> Any producer is at liberty to abstract this
> set if he can still get over the atmosphere.

CHARACTER SKETCHES IN ORDER OF STATIONS

FRANK, Second Chef: *Poultry*. A prisoner of war for four years. Now at thirty-eight he has an easygoing nature. Nothing really upsets him, but then nothing excites him either. He drinks steadily throughout the day and by nightfall is blissfully drunk though instinctively capable. Flirts with the waitresses, squeezing their breasts and pinching their bottoms.

ALFREDO: *Roast*. An old chef, about sixty-five and flat-footed. Large-muscled and strong, though of medium height. He is a typical cook in that he will help nobody and will accept no help; nor will he impart his knowledge. He is the fastest worker there and sets-to straight away, not stopping till his station is all ready. He speaks little, but he has a dry sense of humour. He is the worker and the boss is the boss, and he probably despises the boss. He hums to himself as he works.

HANS: *Fry*. A German boy, nineteen, pimply and adolescent. He is working in London through a system of exchange. He speaks very bad English and is impressed by anything flashy. Yet as a German he is sensitive.

PETER: *Boiled Fish*. Peter is the main character. Another young German, aged twenty-three, who has worked at the Tivoli for the last three years. His parents were killed in the war. He is boisterous, aggressive, too merry, and yet good-natured. After three years at the Tivoli one might say he was living on his nerves. He speaks good English but with an accent, and when he is talking to people he tends to speak into their ear as though he were telling them a secret. It is a nervous moment. A strong characteristic of Peter is his laugh. It is a forced laugh, pronounced 'Hya hya hya,' instead of 'ha ha ha.' He turns this laugh into one of surprise or mockery, derision or simple merriment. There is also a song he sings—music at page 120—which ends in exactly the same laughter. Somehow its maniacal tone is part of the whole atmosphere of the kitchen.

KEVIN: *Fried Fish.* The new young man, Irish, twenty-two. He spends most of his time being disturbed by the mad rush of the work and people around him. This is worse than anything he has ever seen.

GASTON: *Grill.* A Cypriot by birth, forty-odd, slight and dark-complexioned. Everyone-is-his-friend until he starts work, then he is inclined to go to pieces and panic and cry at everyone. When the play starts he has a loud scratch down the side of his face.

MICHAEL: *Eggs.* There is nothing particular about this boy of eighteen. He is what his dialogue will make him; but he is a cook and before long all cooks are infused with a kind of madness.

BERTHA: *Vegetable Cook.* Large woman, coarse, friendly, narrow-minded, Jewish.

MANGOLIS: *Kitchen Porter.* Young Cypriot boy, cheeky, hard-working, dashing in and out of fast-moving kitchen, replenishing plates on hot-plate.

ANNE: *Dessert and Coffee.* Irish, soft-spoken, thirty-five, easy-going. Speaks with slow, cloying lilt.

MAX: *Butcher.* A stout man of fifty. Loud-mouthed, smutty and anti anything that it is easy to be anti about. He has a cigarette continually dropping from his mouth, and like Frank drinks steadily all day till he is drunk.

NICHOLAS: *Cold Buffet.* Nicholas is a young Cypriot who has lived in England three years and can therefore speak reasonable English but with an accent. Speaking the language and working in a capacity socially superior to his compatriots, who are dishwashers, he behaves with a wild heartiness, as one who is accepted. And as one who is accepted he imitates, and he chooses to imitate Frank and Max by becoming drunk by the end of the day.

RAYMOND and PAUL: *Pastrycooks*. Paul is a young Jew; Raymond is an Italian who speaks almost perfect English but with an accent. These two pastrycooks, as opposed to the madmen in the kitchen, are calm and less prone to panic. The rush of the kitchen does not affect them; they work hard and straight through without the afternoon break but have no direct contact with the waitresses. Raymond is emotional. Paul is suave, though not unpleasant.

CHEF: A large man of about fifty-nine with tiny moustache. If he could, he would work elsewhere—preferably not in the catering trade at all. The less that is brought to his attention, the happier he feels. In such a large kitchen the organization carries itself almost automatically. He rarely speaks to any-one except Frank, the second chef, Max, who works near him, and Nicholas, who is immediately under him. He will not say good morning nor communicate any of the politeness expected of a chef. Familiarity, for him, breeds the contempt it deserves.

MR. MARANGO: *Proprietor*. An old man of seventy-five, stout —but not fat—with flabby jowls and a sad expression on his face. A magnificent curtain of grey hair skirts the back of his bald head and curls under itself. His sad look is really one of self-pity. The machine he has set in motion is his whole life and he suspects that everyone is conspiring to stop it.

THE ACTIONS

For the purpose of the action of this play, the following dishes have been allotted to the following cooks. Of course they cannot go through all the actions necessary for the cooking of these dishes. The two important things are:

1 That they have some actions to mime throughout the play in between speaking their parts and gossiping among themselves, and

2 That by the time the service is ready to begin they have an assortment of neatly arranged trays and pots of 'dishes and sauces' ready to serve to the waitresses as requested.

FRANK: Roast pheasant/chips. Roast chicken/pommes sautés. Mushrooms. Pour salt in twenty chicken carcasses, place in oven. Slice carrots and onions and boil for gravy. Salt and place pheasants in oven. (Both carcasses are cleaned elsewhere.) Chop mushrooms and fry together with sauté.

ALFREDO: Roast veal/spaghetti. Boiled ham/boiled potatoes. Roast beef for staff. Season and cook veal and beef in oven. Boil spaghetti in salt water. Chop onions and carrots and make sauce. Place ham in pot to boil.

HANS: Sausages/baked rice. Pork chops/white beans. Vegetables for the staff. Cut up ham, tomatoes, onions and mushrooms, and sauté for rice. Boil white beans. Pork chops are fried during service. Collect from cold cupboard and heat yesterday's vegetables for staff.

PETER: Mixed fish/sauce. Cold meunière/boiled potatoes. Boiled turbot/sauce hollandaise. Beat egg yellows on slow heat, add melted margarine for sauce hollandaise. This takes a long time. Slice cod and turbot into portions. Slice lemons for garniture.

KEVIN: Grilled sardines/boiled potatoes. Grilled salmon/boiled potatoes. Fried plaice/chips or boiled potatoes. Slice lemons for plaice. Cut salmon into portions. Arrange four trays on bench: one for oil, one for milk, one for flour, and one with required fish. Clean grill with wire brush.

GASTON: Grilled chops/chips. Grilled steak/chips. Most of his work is done during service. Clean grill with wire brush. Collect from vegetable-room and then blanch chips. Aid Kevin.

MICHAEL: Hamburger/eggs on top/chips. Ham omelet. Onion

soup. Cut ham for omelet. Cube stale bread for onion soup. Crack eggs in tin ready for omelet. We assume enough soup left over from yesterday.

MAX: Mainly carting of huge meat carcasses from cold-room to bench where he then proceeds to cut and dissect them.

NICHOLAS: Cold roast beef/potato salad. Cold ham/Russian salad. Slice meats and arrange various trays of salad. Also roll and slice in portions chipped meat for Michael's hamburgers.

CHEF: Mainly clerical and organizational work of course. He will mind his own business as much as possible.

PAUL and RAYMOND: Bands of apple and pear tart. Pastry called 'Religieuse'. First bake trays of tarts prepared day before. Spread custard sauce and then slice fruit to lay on top. Make more pastry; mix flour and fat, add water, roll out. Cut into more bands ready for tomorrow. Fill pastry with cream from cloth bag. Peel fruit.

BERTHA: Assume all her vegetables, sprouts, cabbage, spinach and sauté were cooked day before. She merely has to heat them over. Otherwise gossips with coffee woman.

The original, shorter version was first presented by the English Stage Society at the Royal Court Theatre on 13 September 1959. This full-length version was first presented by the English Stage Company at the Royal Court Theatre on 27 June 1961, with the following cast:

MAGI	Tommy Eytle
MAX	Martin Boddey
BERTHA	Jessie Robins
MOLLY	Jane Merrow
WINNIE	Ida Goldapple
MANGOLIS	Marcos Markou
PAUL	Harry Landis
RAYMOND	André Bolton
HETTIE	Rita Tushingham
VIOLET	Alison Bayley
ANNE	Gladys Dawson
GWEN	Jeanne Watts
DAPHNE	Shirley Cameron
CYNTHIA	Sandra Caron
DIMITRI	Dimitri Andreas
BETTY	Tarn Bassett
JACKIE	Charlotte Selwyn
HANS	Wolf Parr
MONIQUE	Mary Peach
ALFREDO	Reginald Green
MICHAEL	James Bolam
GASTON	Andreas Markos
KEVIN	Brian Phelan
NICHOLAS	Andreas Lysandrou
PETER	Robert Stephens
FRANK	Ken Parry
CHEF	Arnold Yarrow
HEAD WAITER	Charles Workman
MARANGO	Andreas Malendrinos
TRAMP	Patrick O'Connell

Directed by John Dexter

PART ONE

There is no curtain in this part. The kitchen is always there. It is semi-darkness. Nothing happens until the audience is quite seated (at the appointed time for commencement, that is).

The night porter, MAGI, enters. He stretches, looks at his watch, and then stands still, realizing where he is. It is seven in the morning. Then with a taper he lights the ovens. Into the first shoots a flame. There is smoke, flame, and soon the oven settles into a steady burn, and with it comes its hum. It is the hum of the kitchen, a small roar. It is a noise that will stay with us to the end. As he lights each oven, the noise grows from a small to a loud ferocious roar. There will be this continuous battle between the dialogue and the noise of the ovens. The Producer must work out his own balance.

As MAGI lights the fourth oven, MAX enters, goes straight to the lower cold cupboard and collects a bottle of beer, which he opens and starts to drink.

As MAGI lights the last oven, BERTHA enters to her station. As she passes MAX she says, 'Good morning, Max.' *He burps.*

BERTHA. Here, Magi, give us a hand with this.

MAGI. O.K., love.

BERTHA. There.

(*Enter* MANGOLIS.)

MAGI. Bertha—that ten shillings.

BERTHA. You haven't got it? So you haven't got it! You going away?

MAGI. No.

BERTHA. Then I'll wait.

MAGI. You're a good girl, Bertha.

BERTHA. Good—I am; but a girl—unfortunately not.

MAGI. Go on. *I* could fancy you.

BERTHA. Me? Boy, I'd crack you in one crush. Crrrrrunch! (*Creeps towards him like a spectre.*) First your arms—snap

snap! Then your legs—snap snap! Then your eyes— gobble! Then your ears and your nose and your throat—gobble gobble gobble!

MAGI. And what would you do with the left-overs?

BERTHA. Kosher it with salt and prayers and hang it up to drip-dry!

MAX. Magi, give us a hand please.

MAGI. Bertha—you worry me.

BERTHA. I worry him.

> (MAX *and* MAGI *raise the beef on to* ALFREDO's *oven. As they do this,* BETTY *and* WINNIE, *waitresses, enter, mumbling, and go through to the dining-room.* PAUL *and* RAYMOND *enter with their tools under their arms. They go to their own corner.* MAGI *exits.*)

PAUL (*to anybody*). Good morning, good morning. (*to* BERTHA) Good morning, me old darling. (*to* MAX) And to you too, Max.

MAX (*his soul not yet returned*). Good morning.

BERTHA. Morning.

RAYMOND. Max, it's escalope of veal on today?

MAX. How many?

RAYMOND. Three. I'll take them now and put them in my box, before the others get there.

> (MAX *goes to cold-room, and returns with three escalopes which he slaps down on his table and* RAYMOND *collects.* MANGOLIS *delivers empty dustbins to their places.*)

MAX. And don't forget my puff pastry tomorrow.

RAYMOND. Usual?

MAX. Usual.

PAUL (*to* RAYMOND *as he returns*). It's Religieuse today?

RAYMOND. Yes. But you do the fruit bands, leave the pastries, I'll do them. Motor bike working all right?

> (HETTIE *and* VIOLET, *waitresses, pass through to the dining-room.*)

HETTIE. This is the way to the dining-room.

VIOLET. I'm not used to working in places like this, I used to be at the old Carlton Tower.

PAUL. Bloody thing! No more second-hand gear for me.

RAYMOND. What is it?

PAUL. If I knew it wouldn't be so bad. Mechanical contraptions! It takes me all my time to find out where the alarm on a clock is.

RAYMOND. I'll look at it.

PAUL. You know about motor bikes?

RAYMOND. In the war I was a dispatch rider—I had to know.

PAUL. I left it at home though.

RAYMOND. I'll come to your home then.

PAUL. I'll make you a supper.

RAYMOND. We'll have an evening of bachelors.

PAUL. A bachelors' evening.

RAYMOND. A bachelors' evening. We'll use the veal cutlets Max promised.

PAUL. Good idea. What about your wife?

RAYMOND. Sometimes it's a good thing to miss a wife.

PAUL. Yes.

RAYMOND. I'm sorry, I forgot.

PAUL. Don't worry on my account—she was a fool. If she'd only been a bitch it wouldn't have mattered but she was a fool as well.

RAYMOND. It's not such a big hurt then?

(*Enter* ANNE *to her station.*)

PAUL. For me? No! But she's going to have children one day and those kids are going to have a fool for a mother—that's what hurts.

RAYMOND. You don't miss her?

PAUL. I don't miss her. Good morning, Anne. (*She doesn't hear.*) Good morning, Anne.

ANNE. Good morning, boys.

PAUL. That's better.

RAYMOND. Good morning, sweetheart.

ANNE. Hello boys, hello Max.

MAX (*his soul returned*). Top o' the mornin' to you, Anne.

ANNE (*putting coffee in metal jug to warm on oven*). An' the rest o' the day to yersel', dear. (*stretching herself*) Ah, me bed was lovely.

RAYMOND (*lasciviously*). I bet it was.

ANNE. Hey, Raymond, tell me, what happened to Peter in the end, you know, last night?

RAYMOND. Now he's a silly boy, eh? Don't you think so? I don't even know what it was all about anyway. You know, Paul?

PAUL. All I know is he had a fight with Gaston. Why? I don't know. Over a ladle I think, or maybe a . . .

MAX. He's a bloody German, a fool, that's what he is. He is always quarrelling, always. There's no one he hasn't quarrelled with, am I right? No one! That's some scheme that is, exchanging cooks! What do we want to exchange cooks for? Three years he's been here, three years! (*Exits to get more beer.*)

ANNE. Ah, the boy's in love.

RAYMOND. What love! You ever see him? When Monique does a turn as hostess by the stairs he watches her through that mirror there. (*Points to glass partition.*)

ANNE. Rubbish.

RAYMOND. And he walks round the kitchen and looks to see if she's talking or flirting with any of the customers.

ANNE. I don't believe it.

BERTHA. Never.

RAYMOND. You don't believe me?

PAUL. And they quarrel in front of everybody as well. They shout at each other. Shout! You know, sometimes she doesn't even look at him, and waits for her orders with her back turned.

ANNE. The poor boy. He's no parents you know. But what happened last night? I want to know.

(MAGI *re-enters.*)

MAX. Ask Magi.

MAGI. Any coffee, Anne?

ANNE. Sure dear. (*Pours.*) Help yourself.

RAYMOND. Hey Magi, what happened with Peter last night, uh?

MAGI (*unconcerned*). They nearly killed him.

ANNE. Oh God.

RAYMOND (*gesticulating*). But what was it all about, tell me? I don't know nothing, me.

MAGI. Well *you* should know that—I wasn't here.

PAUL. All we know is that they suddenly started shouting at each other. And you know, Peter always shouts more than the other and you can always hear Peter—well, so then it stopped, and then a few seconds later they were fighting, and I saw Gaston raise a boning knife and Peter knock it out of his hand, and then . . .

RAYMOND. And then he lifted him and nearly sat him on the stove and...

PAUL. And then the Chef came along and . . .

ANNE. Well I saw the Chef separate them and I heard Gaston say 'I haven't finished yet, it's not over yet,' but I still don't know what it was all about.

PAUL. Who cares? I say good morning to Peter but never good night.

MAGI. Well I came in at nine last night. The boys were changing and suddenly Peter comes and Gaston follows him. Gaston says Peter called him a lousy Cypro and the boys make circle round him and want to murder him! All of them . . . but Peter says 'No, everyone for me is the same—it makes no difference race, you misunderstand . . .' They all wanted to hit him! And he was scared! I never seen him so white.

ANNE. But what was it about to begin with?

MAX. A ladle, I tell you.

PAUL. Who knows? There's always fights, who knows how they begin?

MAGI (*laying down cup*). Well, I'm going.

PAUL. Have a good kip, old son.

ANNE. And I must get started too. (*Looks round empty kitchen.*) You wouldn't think this place will become a madhouse in two hours, would you now. (*Moves off with* MAGI.)

(RAYMOND, PAUL *and* MAX *continue to work in silence. Enter* DAPHNE, GWEN *and* CYNTHIA, *waitresses, to dining-room.*)

DAPHNE. So if he doesn't come home tonight I'm going to leave.

CYNTHIA. Well he does have to work in the afternoon.

GWEN. That's right.

MAX. Any luck on the pools, Ray?

RAYMOND. Huh!

MAX. Norwich and Leyton let me down. Twenty points. Twenty points!

(*Enter* HETTIE *from dining-room for a coffee. Pause.*)

HETTIE. Morning, Annie love.

PAUL. Read about the man in the mental home who won thirty-five thousand pounds?

RAYMOND. And his wife turned up after eighteen years?

(*Enter* DAPHNE *from dining-room for a coffee.*)

PAUL. Eighteen years!

(*Pause.* DIMITRI *enters. A Cypriot kitchen porter, young, good-looking and intelligent. He is carrying in his hand a home-made portable radio. He is happy as he takes it to* PAUL. *He speaks with an accent.*

Enter MOLLY *and* JACKIE, *waitresses, to dining-room.*)

DIMITRI. I make it Paul, I make it. There! (*Lays it on table near by.*) She does not look handsome. I'm sorry for that.

PAUL. Ah you good boy, Dimitri. Can we play it? (*He looks round to see if authority is in sight. Only* DAPHNE *and* HETTIE *approach. One has a bucket in her hand and her hair is tied up with a scarf. The other one is similarly attired and carries a feather duster.*) Anyone around?

HETTIE (*pointing to portable*). What is it, Paul?

PAUL. Is Marango around yet?

DAPHNE. Not yet. Whose is it?

PAUL. It's mine. Dimitri here made it.

RAYMOND. You made it on your own? All those little wires and plugs? Tell me, what are you doing here? Why you waste your time with dishes in this place? You can't get a job in a factory?

DIMITRI. A factory? You think I find happiness in a factory? What I make there? Uh? This little wire, you see it? This I would make, or that . . . what you call it?

PAUL. Knob.

DIMITRI. Knob. That perhaps I could put in. All day I would screw in knobs. I tell you, in a factory a man makes a little piece till he becomes a little piece, you know what I mean?

HETTIE. It's true, he's right, you know.

DIMITRI. Sure I know, my brother, he works there. I know all right.

RAYMOND. Hey Dimitri, *you* know what happened to Peter last night?

DIMITRI. They nearly kill him. Why?

DAPHNE. Oh my Gawd.

DIMITRI. But you think it was all Peter's fault? They all wanted to fight. Listen, you put a man in the plate-room all day, he's got dishes to make clean, and stinking bins to take away, and floors to sweep, what else there is for him to do— he wants to fight. He got to show he is a man some way. So—blame him!

(DIMITRI *turns on the radio, which plays a loud rock 'n' roll tune.* PAUL *grabs* DAPHNE, *and starts to dance,* HETTIE *tries to dance with* DIMITRI, *who won't . . .* HANS *enters, grabs* HETTIE, *they dance. At the height of the dance,* MONIQUE *enters from the dining-room.*)

MONIQUE. Marango's in the dining-room.

ALL. What!

MONIQUE. Marango's in the dining-room.

> (*There is a scramble to restore everything to normal, work is resumed,* DIMITRI *vanishes into the plate-room with the radio.* HANS *exits.*
>
> *Enter* ALFREDO.)

ALFREDO. It's only me. Good morning, gentlemen.

MAX (*pointing to* ALFREDO'S *station*). The veal is there.

ALFREDO (*studying the menu on the board*). Thank you, thank you.

PAUL (*shouting*). Is the new cook here?

ALFREDO (*shrugging his shoulders*). He didn't ask for me.

> (*Enter* MONIQUE *with glasses.*)

PAUL. I thought you said Marango's coming.

MONIQUE. I said he's in the dining-room—he's still there.

RAYMOND. Monique, what happened last night, you tell us?

MONIQUE. No more Ray, there's a good man. Gaston has a black eye.

PAUL. A right morning we're going to have this morning then.

RAYMOND. A Peter—nothing?

MONIQUE. He was lucky.

RAYMOND. You mean he was with you so they couldn't touch him.

MONIQUE. I mean he was lucky. They waited for him outside.

RAYMOND. Outside also?

MONIQUE. 'You want to play gangsters?' he says to them, 'Go bring me Marlon Brando and I'll play gangsters.'

RAYMOND. A time like that he's funny.

MONIQUE. And then he shakes hands with them and says 'Good night, bonne nuit, gute Nacht and Kalinka' one by one. And he leaves them all standing. (*Smiles.*) What could they do? (*Smile fades.*) The bully!

HEAD WAITER. Monique . . . (*As he enters from dining-room.*)

MONIQUE. Morning, Harry.

HEAD WAITER. Janey is sick.

MONIQUE. Not again. That girl's anaemic, I swear she's anaemic.

HEAD WAITER. Take over for the day, please.

MONIQUE. But I'm not dressed for hostess.

HEAD WAITER. That dress looks all right to me—just take off the apron.

MONIQUE. This one? But it's not ironed!

HEAD WAITER. You only have to show the customers to their tables, not dance with them. (*Exits.*)

MONIQUE. That's three times this week I've been hostess. Here Bertha, look after this apron for me.

BERTHA. Give it me Tchooch, I'll sit on it and keep it pressed. (*Enter* DAPHNE, GWEN *and* HETTIE.)

MONIQUE. Hettie, Janey's sick again, take over my station, will you love? Daphne, give her a hand will you?

DAPHNE. I'm on glasses don't forget.

MONIQUE. True ... I forgot. Who's left then? Winnie's on ten. Gwen's on ... Gwen, what station you on today?

GWEN. Seven.

MONIQUE. Seven. . . . That's your hands full.

HETTIE. What about the new woman.

MONIQUE. That's marvellous, she's an old hand isn't she? She can help you, and you can keep an eye on her—come on, let's move.

PAUL. And the best of British luck.

MONIQUE. At least it means I won't have to stand in front of that bully all day.

(*The waitresses all exit.*)

PAUL. Fancy that sort of relationship.

RAYMOND. Peter and Monique? They're not so bad—it's her husband I wouldn't like to be.

PAUL. No, you wouldn't.

RAYMOND. There—I've done it again. I'm sorry Paul.

PAUL. That's all right, I don't mind being cuckolded, I'm in good company.

(*Enter* MICHAEL.)

MICHAEL (*to* BERTHA). Morning, fatty, How are you?

BERTHA. And you can shut up for a start, little boy. I can ring your napkins out any day. With you tucked in them, any day.

(*Enter* GASTON.)

MICHAEL (*to* GASTON). Your eye's black.

GASTON. YOU TELLING ME SOMETHING.

MICHAEL. All right, all right . . . whew. . . . He looked as though he wanted to kill me.

PAUL. Who'd want to kill you, Michael?

MICHAEL. Quite right . . . who'd want to kill me? Young man in his teens, all the world in front of him. Look at it . . . a lovely sight, isn't it? Isn't she beautiful? A bloody great mass of iron and we work it—praise be to God for man's endeavour—what's on the menu today? I don't know why I bother—it's always the same. Vegetable soup, minestrone, omolleteeee au jambon—ah well! One day I'll work in a place where I can create masterpieces, master bloody pieces. Beef Stroganoff, Chicken Kiev, and that king of the Greek dishes—Mousaka.

GASTON. Never. You'll never create a Mousaka. Chips you can make—chips with everything.

MICHAEL. Don't you think you Greek's have got the monopoly on good cooking, you know. There was a time when the English knew how to eat.

GASTON. There was a time.

MICHAEL. Aye—well—yes—there was a time.

(*Enter* HANS, *who escorts* KEVIN. *Sooner or later they all arrive to glance at the menu on the blackboard.* NICHOLAS *follows them to his station.*)

HANS (*to* KEVIN). I not know where you work. On fish perhaps.

(*to* PAUL) Paul, new cook.

PAUL. Hello.

(*They continue to work while* KEVIN *watches them and the rest of the kitchen.*)

KEVIN. Is there much doing here?

PAUL. You'll see. Two thousand customers a day.

(*While* KEVIN *has been introduced and is talking to the pastrycooks,* BERTHA *goes to the cold cupboard and, after looking around inside, takes out a tray of sliced, cold potatoes. Following behind, about to start his work, is* NICHOLAS. *He has a bottle of beer in his hand, which he is drinking.*)

NICHOLAS (*to* BERTHA). Where you go with that?

BERTHA. I need it for sauté.

NICHOLAS (*taking tray*). Oh, no, no, no. That's for me. Me, I prepared that yesterday. That's for me for my salad.

BERTHA (*trying to hold on to tray*). You get your salad from the vegroom.

NICHOLAS. Ah no bloody hell! You get *yours* from the veg. That is for me, that is what I get ready.

BERTHA (*nastily*). You don't bloody hell me, my son. You bloody hell in your own country. (*to others*) What d'you think of him, eh? The little . . .

NICHOLAS. This is my country.

BERTHA. The lavatory is your country.

NICHOLAS (*taking tray eventually*). The lavatory is *your* country, and the sewers, you know that? The sewers.

BERTHA (*taking out another tray*). I'll pay you sonny. You cross me once, that's all, just once. Lousy little foreigner you!

NICHOLAS (*cheekily*). *She* calls *me* foreigner! Listen to her . . .

ALFREDO (*approaching cupboard for his own goods*). Excuse me friends, you can carry on in a minute. (*But the quarrel has died down.*)

NICHOLAS (*approaching pastry-section*). D'you hear her? Uh? The cow! Paul, you got some tart or cake or something? I'm starving. (PAUL *hands him tart.*) (*to* KEVIN) You the new cook?

KEVIN. Yes.

NICHOLAS. Good luck to you! (*Laughs to the others.*) You know where your station is?

KEVIN. I don't even know what stations there are.

NICHOLAS. Here, I'll show you. Right now for a start there's the menu. . . . That's where you find what to cook for day, our chef writes it out each night. Over here, this is where I work on the Cold Buffet. This is Max the Butcher. This is where Hans works, he does Staff and rice and cutlets and you know, and this is Alfredo on the Roast. And next here, we got the Second Chef Frank on Poultry. . . . And here, well here you see that fat bitch down there, well she works here as the Veg Cook. And this is my Aunty Anne who is on the teas and coffees. This is Michael on Soups and Omelets. And this is my best friend Gaston, the best cook in this kitchen, he does steaks and chops. Co-Co works here but he's off today. Here are Paul and Raymondo, Pastrycooks. And here, this is where Peter works on Boiled Fish, he . . .

(*By this time he has to take* KEVIN *back to left of stage and point out the other stations. As he talks on,* PETER *enters in a great hurry, he is late. He laughs his laugh.*)

PETER. Auf geht's! Auf geht's!

HANS. Auf geht's, Pete! Was war denn los heut' Morgen?

PETER. Ach, die Weiber! Die Weiber!

NICHOLAS. Peter, the new cook, I give him to you.

PETER. So what shall I do with him? (*to* KEVIN) You know where it is you work?

KEVIN. Not yet I don't.

PETER. Where do you come from?

KEVIN. Ireland.

PETER. No, I mean what restaurant you work in before?

KEVIN. Parisito. Shaftesbury Avenue.

PETER (*rubbing his thumb and finger together*). Good pay?

KEVIN (*shaking his head*). That's why I came here.

PETER. Oh, you get good money here—but you work! (*raising his hands in despair*) Oh yes! Now, you help me. Can you make a sauce hollandaise? You know—eggs and . . . (*Makes motion of whisking.*)

KEVIN. Yes, yes.

PETER (*briskly*). The eggs are already in a tin in the cold cupboard. There is a pot, the whisk is in the drawer and I melt margarine for you.

(*By now almost everybody is working. Waitresses are making an appearance, they are carrying glasses back and forth; one, CYNTHIA, is handing out the printed menu for the day, another is taking round bread for lunch for the kitchen staff. As she reaches HANS, he approaches her shyly and tries to flirt with her.*)

HANS. Oh baby, wait a moment! I . . . I . . . I . . . Du gefällst mir, du hast mir schon vom ersten Tag an gefallen! Könnten wir nicht mal was zusammen arrangieren?

(FRANK, *the second chef, enters and breaks up conversation.*)

MAX (*to* FRANK). We got no lamb cutlets.

FRANK. Three carcasses came in yesterday.

MAX. So?

FRANK. So!

MAX. So you come and help me cut them up. I'm on my own today.

FRANK. What you got?

MAX. Veal cutlets.

FRANK. O.K., so veal cutlets then. (*moving to* KEVIN) New cook?

KEVIN (*sweating and still beating his sauce*). Yes, Chef.

FRANK. Right, you work on the fried fish this morning.

PETER (*approaching from cutting-table*). Thank you, thank you, but I got six dishes to prepare.

FRANK. Co-Co is off today. Someone must do the fry.

PETER. Bloody house this is. The middle of summer and we got no staff. I got six dishes.

(*The* CHEF *enters.*)

ALFREDO. Morning, Chefie.

CHEF. Morning.

MAX. Morning, Chef.

CHEF. Morning.

HANS (*cheekily*). Morning, Chefie.

> (*The* CHEF *stops, turns, looks* HANS *up and down, then continues to his desk.* HANS *pulls a face, and makes a rude sign.*)

FRANK. Morning, Leo. (*to* KEVIN) Here, you, get that fish out of that cupboard and come here, I want to show you something.

HANS (*to* PETER). Du, gestern Abend hat's dich aber beinah erwischt!

PETER. Sie sind nur mutig, wenn sie zusammen sind!

HANS. Haben sie draussen auf dich gewartet?

PETER. Ja, da warin auch welche. Leider war ich mit Monika zusammen und jetzt spricht sie nicht mehr mit mir.

HANS. Sie wird auch wieder mit dir reden!

PETER. Ach egal! Auf geht's! (*Sings his song, in which* HANS *joins him, ending in laughter.*) Hi lee, hi lo, hi la!

GASTON (*passing at that moment*). Madmen, lunatics!

PETER. Hey Gaston, I'm sorry—your black eye, I'm sorry about it.

GASTON. DON'T TALK TO ME.

PETER. I say I'm sorry, that's all.

GASTON. You sorry because half a dozen Cypriot boys make you feel sorry—but we not finished yet!

PAUL. Gaston! What's the matter with you? A man is saying sorry—so accept!

GASTON. Accept? He gives me this (*pointing to black eye*) and I must accept? (*to* PETER) We not finished yet, I'm telling you.

PETER. What you not finished with? Tell me! What you want to do now? You want to give me a black eye? That make you feel happier? All right! Here, give me one and then we'll be finished, eh? (*Adopts quixotic stance.*)

GASTON. Don't laugh, Peter, I'm telling you, it gets worse, don't laugh.

(PETER *adopts another quixotic stance.*)

PAUL (*to* PETER). So what are you tantalizing him for? Lunatic! (*to* RAYMOND) Nobody knows when to stop. A quarrel starts and it goes on for months. When *one* of them is prepared to apologize so the other doesn't know how to accept—and when someone knows how to accept so the other . . . ach! Lunatics! (*Throws a hand of disgust, while* PETER *sings loudly.*)

(MONIQUE *approaches* GASTON *and lays a friendly arm on his shoulder as they both watch* PETER'S *antics.*)

MONIQUE. He makes a lot of noise but he's not really dangerous.

GASTON. Listen to him—your boy-friend!

MONIQUE. Show me the eye. Beautiful! First prize!

GASTON. Now Monique, don't protect him.

MONIQUE. But you know he wouldn't hurt anyone—not intentionally.

GASTON. This eye—

MONIQUE. It was an accident, you know it was, just between us you know it was, don't you? Why don't you just let me try and handle him?

GASTON. You? You're like a bit of paper—the wind blows you about.

MONIQUE. I manage.

GASTON. Manage? What sort of a life is manage? Manage! He needs a big scare, a big fright.

MONIQUE. Fright? Nothing frightens that boy.

GASTON. Boy! A baby! You just threaten to leave him and you'll see how frightened he'll get. Listen to him—baby!

(*The* HEAD WAITER *enters to* CHEF'*s desk.*)

HEAD WAITER (*handing* CHEF *a letter*). Read it.

CHEF. What's this one about?

HEAD WAITER. Read it. Read it.

CHEF. Sour soup, what sour soup?

HEAD WAITER. Yesterday's.

CHEF. I was off yesterday, see Frank.

HEAD WAITER. He was off yesterday . . . A kitchen he runs. (*Goes to* FRANK.)

FRANK. What do you want? Nicholas! Twelve chickens.

NICHOLAS. There are only six.

FRANK. Well order some more! What's this sour soup . . . ?

HANS. Ahf geht's, Nicholas! Come on, Nicholas! Twelve chickens, please! Bonjour Raymond, comment ça va?

RAYMOND. Ça va, toujours au boulot, etcetera.

HANS. Vive le frigue!

MAX (*suddenly and violently to* HANS). You're in England now, speak bloody English. (HANS *is nonplussed for the day.*) Everybody speaking in a different language, French, Italian, German. (*to* HANS) You come here to learn English didn't you? Well speak it then!

PETER. What's the matter, Max? You frightened of something? Have another beer.

MAX. I'm not frightened of you, I tell you that straight. So *you* can keep quiet.

PETER (*approaching close to* MAX *and talking in his ear*). You know your trouble, Max? You been here too long.

MAX (*moving away from him*). Yes, yes, yes Peter, all right.

PETER (*following him*). How long have you been here? Twenty-one years? You need a change.

MAX (*moving away again*). Yes, yes.

PETER (*following him*). Why don't you go work a season in Germany?

MAX. Sure to.

PETER. Visit other kitchens! Learn more!

MAX. Yes, yes, Get on with your work.

PETER. Don't you worry about my work!

HANS. Genug, Pete.

PETER. You can't bear a change? A new face upsets you?

MAX. Let's drop it? Erwigt yes?

HANS. Stop it, Pete!

CHEF. All right, Peter—let's have some work!

(MR. MARANGO *appears*.)

HANS. Marango!!

(PETER *returns to his work and winks at* RAYMOND *in passing*. MARANGO *walking slowly round the kitchen inspecting everything, placing his hand on the hot-plate to see if it is still working. It is a mechanical movement—sometimes he puts a hand on the cold pastry slab to see if it is still hot—it is a mechanical tour. Meanwhile—*)

KEVIN (*to* PETER). Is it like this every day? (*wiping sweat from forehead*) Look at me, I never sweated so much since me glorious honeymoon.

PETER. It is nothing this. This is only how it begins. Wait till we start serving, then. (*Raises his hands*.) You in place?

KEVIN. More or less. I got me salmon to cut.

PETER. Good, we eat soon.

MARANGO (*gently to* KEVIN). You're the new cook?

KEVIN (*wiping his brow again*). Yes sir.

MARANGO. It's hot eh, son?

KEVIN. Sure, an' a bit more.

MARANGO. Never mind, I pay you well. Just work, that's all, just work well. (*Continues tour*.)

KEVIN (*to* PETER). He seems a kind old man.

PETER. You think he is kind? He is a bastard! He talks like that because it is summer now. Not enough staff to serve all his customers, that is why he is kind. You going to stay till winter? Wait till then. You'll see. The fish is burnt! Too much mise-en-place! The soup is sour! He is a man, he is a restaurant. I tell you. He goes to market at five thirty in the morning; returns here, reads the mail, goes up to the office and then comes down here to watch the service. Here he stands, sometimes he walks round touching the hot-plate, closing the hot-plate doors, then looking inside this thing and that thing. Till the last customer he stays. Then he has a sleep upstairs in his office. Half an hour after we come back, he is here again—till nine thirty, maybe ten at night. Every day, morning to night. What kind of a life is that, in a kitchen! Is that a life I ask you? Me, I don't care, soon I'm going to get married and then whisht—(*Makes movement with his arm to signify 'I'm off'*.)

HANS (*approaches with large tray in his hand which he later puts in cold cupboard*). Auf geht's, Irishman! I must not speak German to you. I'm in England and have to speak *bloody* English. Hi lee, hi lo, hi la!

(*At this point,* MONIQUE *passes by where* PETER *is working. She is carrying glasses.*)

MONIQUE (*to* PETER). Bully!

PETER (*to* MONIQUE). Go to hell! (*to* KEVIN *proudly*) That's my wife, or she will be soon. Look (*takes out card from wallet*)—this card she sent me when she was on holiday. (*reading aloud*) 'I am not happy till you come. I love you very much.' And look, her lipstick marks. She is very lovely, yes?

KEVIN. She looks like a girl I knew, all bosom and bouncing you know?

PETER (*not really understanding what* KEVIN *said*). We eat soon, eh? (KEVIN *goes off to pursue his printed menu.*) (*to* HANS) Hans, hilf mir. (*They take a large heavy pot off from the oven, and pass the contents through a strainer into a small pot which* PETER *has prepared on the ground.*)

KEVIN (*showing menu to* PETER). Look here, it says on the printed menu fried plaice and on the board it says fried sole.

PETER. See the Chef.

KEVIN (*approaching* CHEF). Good morning, Chef. Look, it says here fried plaice and on the board it's got fried sole.

CHEF. I don't know anything about it. It was my day off yesterday, see the Second Chef.

KEVIN. Have we got any plaice?

CHEF (*sarcastically looking inside his apron*). It's not here.

KEVIN (*moves away to* RAYMOND). Now that's a helpful person for you. Doesn't he care about anything?

RAYMOND. He don't want to know nothing, only when it's gone wrong.

> (MONIQUE *again passes in front of* PETER *to glassery.* PETER *is angry. Tries to make his quarrel secret but of course this is impossible.*)

PETER. Why do you still call me bully, all day you call me bully.

MONIQUE (*moves away across front of stage*). Bully!

PETER (*following her and talking, as is his habit, in her ear*). You think to make me angry? What is it you wanted me to do? Let him fight me?

MONIQUE (*turning to him at last*). He's got a black eye now you see?

PETER. I see, I see. But he raised a knife to me.

MONIQUE. Bully. (*She turns away.*)

PETER (*following her like the pathetic, jealous lover*). And remember you're hostess today, I can see you in the glass. No flirting, do you hear? (*Grips her arm.*) No flirting.

MONIQUE. I shall talk to who I like. (*Moves off.*)

PETER (*hoping no one can hear him*). Cow! Disgusting cow! All the restaurant can see you.

> (*At this point,* HANS *draws out the table from the pastry-section more to the centre of the stage, and begins to lay it with cutlery and glasses and bread, ready for lunch.* MAX, ALFREDO, NICHOLAS *and* FRANK *prepare to eat at* MAX's *table.* KEVIN, MICHAEL, PETER *and* HANS *will eat at the table* HANS *is now laying.* GASTON *will not eat because he will not sit with* PETER. *These two continue to ignore each other throughout the day.*)

MICHAEL (*shouting*). Who has the strainer? Gaston? Peter?

PETER. I got it here, you'll have to clean it. (*to a kitchen porter who is near by*) Hey, Mangolis, you clean this for Michael please?

(MANGOLIS *makes a rude sign with his hand and moves off.*
PETER *shrugs his shoulder,* and MICHAEL *heaves up strainer
himself, and carts it off.* HETTIE *stops in her work to speak
to* PETER.)

HETTIE (*as though to confide in her only*). Hey, Peter, what
happened last night, they didn't . . . ?

PETER (*briskly, as she only wants to gossip*). No, no, Cowards,
all of them. It was nothing.

PAUL (*to same waitress as she passes his section*). Hettie, did you
go last night?

HETTIE (*ecstatically*). Mmm.

PAUL. He's a good actor?

HETTIE (*even more ecstatically and hugging herself*). What a
man. Oh one night, just one night with him, and then I wash
dishes all my life. (*Moves off.*)

RAYMOND (*to* PAUL). So what chance do we stand? You
wonder my wife doesn't make love like she used to?

PAUL. And that's why I'm not going to get married. I buy
picture books and I'm happy.

GWEN. All right boys, staff meal, coming up.

(*While* PAUL *and* RAYMOND *are talking, a long procession
of straggling, gossiping and giggling waitresses have come
down stage on the left and are moving around to* HANS *and*
ALFREDO, *who have laid trays of food on the serving-
counters. Beside food are piles of plates. The waitresses help
themselves.*)

GWEN. What've you got for us this morning?

ALFREDO. Curried cats and dogs.

GWEN. Is this cabbage from yesterday?

HANS. It's all right, it's all right, eat it, eat.

VIOLET. What are these?

HANS. Very good, very good. Cauliflower and white sauce.

VIOLET. White sauce? It smells.

MOLLY. Got anything good, Hans?

HANS. If you don't like—go to Chef.

MOLLY. Got any boiled potatoes?

HANS. Not cooked yet, not ready, ach . . .

> (HANS *moves away in disgust leaving them to serve themselves. He watches* PETER *working a second, and then goes into steam-room. As the waitresses are serving themselves and grumbling and eventually moving off to the dining-room, we discover that* NICHOLAS *has been arguing with* DAPHNE. *He is making his quarrel much too public for her liking. He is probably a little drunk already.*)

NICHOLAS. Me? Me? Me a liar?

DAPHNE. Yes, you.

NICHOLAS. Oh! So I lied when I say I pass the catering exams, eh? I lie when I say I got a rise, eh? I lie when I say I got us a flat, eh? I always *do* and you always say I don't. That's a good marriage is it?

DAPHNE. You're not satisfied? Move!

NICHOLAS. Well listen to that twist! Listen-to-that-woman's-twisting! Come and ask him then, come on. You don't believe *me*, believe *him* then.

DAPHNE. No, Nicky, no . . . now stop.

NICHOLAS. Well, why don't you believe me then? If I tell you I got to stay the afternoon, why don't you believe me? (*shouting*) Frank! Frank! Where is he now. (*Wanders off in search of Frank while waitress waits wondering what he is going to do.*)

RAYMOND (*shouting to waitress*). Hit him! Go on, you're big enough. (*Nudges* PAUL, *they laugh.*)

FRANK (*as he is dragged into the scene by* NICHOLAS). What do you want me for? What is it now, eh?

DAPHNE. Oh Nicky, don't be a fool. (*to* RAYMOND *and* PAUL *despairingly*) Oh for Christ's sake, what do you think of him now!

NICHOLAS. No, ask him, go on. You don't believe me.

FRANK. Ask him what, for hell's sake?

NICHOLAS. Have I got to work in the afternoon or haven't I?

FRANK (*moving away, incredulous that he has been called away for this*). You called me for *that*? You mad or something? Do me a favour and leave me out of this, will you. (*grinning to the others*) Asks me to solve his marriage problems. (*to* NICHOLAS) I'll tell you how to do it as well, ha, ha, ha!

(*Crashing in on laughter is a loud scream from the steam-room.* HANS *comes running out with his hands covering his face. A number of people run and crowd him.*)

HANS. My face! My face! I burnt my face.

FRANK. What is it, Hans?

HANS. Who bloody fool put a pot of hot water on steamer?

PETER. It fell on you?

HANS (*moving away from crowd*). Bastard house! I never worked before so bad. Never, never... (PETER *takes him away for some first aid.*)

FRANK. He'll live. (*to the crowd*) All right, it's all over, come on. (*Crowd disperses.* FRANK *moves over to* CHEF.)

MOLLY (*calling after them*). Put some of that yellow stuff on him.

FRANK. No matter how many times you tell them they still rush around.

CHEF (*he is not interested, shrugs shoulders*). Is the new chap all right?

FRANK. He seems to be. Look out. (MARANGO *approaches.*)

MARANGO. What happened to the boy?

CHEF (*as though concerned*). I don't know. I wasn't there. Frank, what happened?

FRANK (*wearily*). Someone left a pot of boiling water on one of the steamers and he tipped it over his face.

MARANGO. He's burnt his face. It's not serious, (*to* CHEF) but it might have been. (*He shakes his head sadly and moves away.*)

CHEF. What can I do, Mr. Marango? They rush about like mad, I tell them but they don't listen.

(MARANGO *moves off shaking his head still.*)

CHEF (*to* FRANK). Much he cares. It interrupts the kitchen so he worries. Three more years, Frank, three, that's all and then the whisht! Retire, finish! Then you can take over.

FRANK. Oh no! Not this boy. I'm in charge one day a week— enough! They can find another madman.

CHEF. Do you think I'm mad?

FRANK. Do you enjoy your work?

CHEF. Who does?

FRANK. So on top of not enjoying your work you take on responsibility—that isn't mad?

CHEF. I've got a standard of living to keep up—idiot!

FRANK (*moving off*). So go mad!

CHEF. Idiot! Michael!

MICHAEL. Chef?

CHEF. The soup was sour yesterday.

MICHAEL. Sour?

CHEF. Sour!

MICHAEL. But it was only a day old.

CHEF. I've had letters from customers.

MICHAEL. Customers!

CHEF. And Michael—don't take chickens home with you.

MICHAEL. Chickens?

CHEF. Take cutlets, take cold meats but not chickens. Chickens are bulky. Wait till you're my age before trying chickens.

MICHAEL. Oh, I must graduate to it like.

CHEF. That's right, you must graduate to it like. You can have your lunch now.

(PETER *and* HANS *return.*)

KEVIN. You all right?

(HANS *makes a movement of his hands to say 'Ach, I'm fed-up, forget it.'*)

PAUL. You look beautiful.

KEVIN. A Red Indian.

PETER. Come on, let's eat.

(*They all move to their places to eat:* PAUL *returns to his work; there is less activity in the kitchen now—the calm before the storm. A few waitresses wander around, a porter sweeps the floor.*)

KEVIN (*to* PETER). How long have you been here?

PETER. Three years.

(MICHAEL *laughs.*)

KEVIN. How did you stick it?

MICHAEL. Sick all ready?

KEVIN. I don't think I'll last the day.

PETER. People are always coming and going.

HANS (*he is not eating much*). I think me I'll go soon.

MICHAEL (*to* KEVIN). The worse is to come. (*to others*) Am I right? You wait till the service, ah! . . . But you'll get used to it after a while.

PETER. We all said we wouldn't last the day, but tell me what is there a man can't get used to? Nothing! You just forget where you are and you say it's a job.

MICHAEL. He should work on the eggs. Five dishes I've got, five! Hey Paul, any cakes?

PAUL. They're all gone—I got some tart from yesterday. (*raising his shoulders*) Sorry!

MICHAEL (*not too loudly*). Liar!

KEVIN. I thought you could eat what you liked here.

MICHAEL. You can, but you have to swipe it. Even the food for cooking. If I want to make an onion soup that's any good, I go to the cold-room and I take some chickens' wings to make my stock. No questions, just in and out—whisht!

PAUL (*to* RAYMOND). Why do we say there isn't any cake when there is?

RAYMOND. Don't you worry—they eat plenty.

PAUL. So do we. Have you ever caught yourself saying something you don't mean to say? Why did I refuse Michael a cake? Doesn't hurt me to give him a cake, most times we do but there's always that one time when we don't. First thing in the morning I joke with him and half way through the day I lie to him, defending the governor's property as though it was me own. I don't know what to be bloody loyal to half the time.

PETER. Hey, where's Gaston? Why is he not with us, eating here? I black his eye not his arse.

PAUL. Leave off, Peter—the row's over now, patch it up.

MICHAEL. When husbands and wives can't patch up their rows, who are we to succeed?

PAUL. My wife was a mean-minded woman, Michael. She came from a well-run and comfortable-off home but she was mean-minded. I did right by her so don't you be concerned about that. (FRANK, ALFREDO *and* MAX *laugh amongst themselves.*) Every time someone asked us how we were she used to say 'Busybody'. Oh yes you can laugh, cocker, but I used to have to spend hours listening to her being bitchy about other women. I tried everything. Hours I spent—I even tried to—aaah what the hell do I bother to explain to you for, here—take your bloody bit of cake.

(*Embarrassed silence.*)

HANS. I think I go to America.

KEVIN. America?

HANS (*grins sheepishly, he is about to surprise* KEVIN). I been to New York already.

KEVIN. You have?

HANS. I already been twice. (*Nods head to say 'What do you think of that!'*) Worked on a ship. (*Pause.*) On a ship you waste more than you eat. (*Lets this sink in.*) You throw everything into the sea before you come on land. (*Sinks in further.*) Whole chickens! The gulls, you know, they eat it.

KEVIN. What about New York?

HANS (*kissing his fingers*). New York? New York, das ist die schönste Stadt der Welt! Wenn du ankommst—When you arrive: The skyline! The Empire State Buildings! Coney Island! And Broadway, Broadway—you heard of Broadway? (KEVIN *nods with his mouth full.*) Ah . . . beautiful city.

KEVIN. I heard it, yes.

HANS (*in his stride now. Grimace, meaning—'No question of it !'*). And Kevin! Women! Three in the morning! And bars and night-clubs! Rush here and rush there! (*More grimace. Secretly, the others jeer good-naturedly.*) A beautiful city! I think this house not very good . . . here.

KEVIN. It's not, eh?

PETER (*moving to get glass of water*). You got to turn out food hot and quickly. Quality—pooh! No time!

KEVIN. Even in the small restaurants they're not after caring much.

MICHAEL (*lighting cigarette*). Why should they! It's this (*rubs thumb and finger together*) that counts, you know that.

KEVIN. Oh I don't know. You'd've thought it was possible to run a small restaurant that could take pride in its food and made money too.

PETER. Of course it's possible, my friend—but you pay to eat in it. It's money. It's all money. The world chase money so you chase money too. (*snapping his fingers in a lunatic way*) Money! Money! Money!

(PETER *is now near* FRANK. *On an impulse he places glass in the cup of* FRANK's *tall white hat, and creeps back laughing his laugh to himself.*)

PETER. Frank!

(FRANK *of course moves and the water spills over him. More laughter from* PETER.)

FRANK (*shouting across to* PETER). One day you'll lay an egg too many and it'll crack under you. Yes—you laugh.

PETER. Frank is also unhappy. (GWEN *approaches table.*) Yes?

GWEN (*lays hand on* MICHAEL's *shoulder; he lays his on her buttocks*). Who's on fish today?

MICHAEL. Do you love me?

GWEN. I think you're irresistible. Who's on fish?

KEVIN. Me.

GWEN. Right, I order four plaice. (*Moves off.*)

PETER (*easing* KEVIN *back to seat because he has just risen to serve that order*). You got time. You not finished your lunch yet. The customer can wait. (*to* KEVIN) Be like Mr. Alfredo. Nothing disturbs Mr. Alfredo. Mr. Alfredo is a worker and he hates his boss. He knows his job but he does no more no less and at the right time. Mr. Alfredo is an Englishman— look at that!

> (*At this point* MR. ALFREDO *comes to the front of the stage and looks around to see that no one is watching. No one is. He tucks something first into the right of his apron. Then, straightening himself out he returns to pick his teeth.* MOLLY *approaches* FRANK.)

MOLLY. Mr. Marango wants a leg of chicken and some sauté.

FRANK. Mr. Marango can go to hell, I'm eating.

MOLLY (*moves off*). I'll call for it in five minutes.

FRANK. They don't give you a chance to eat here.

MAX. Hey, you heard they nearly killed Peter last night?

FRANK. Don't talk to me about that boy. He's mad. I've had too much of him already . . . three years.

NICHOLAS. They should kill 'em off! Kill 'em off! The lot! Boche! I hate them, you know! I don't hate no one like I hate them. And they want to abolish hanging now. You read about it?

MAX (*to* FRANK). Do you think that Bill'll go through?

FRANK. How should I know! I suppose it's worth a try.

MAX. They'll be sorry, I'm telling you.

NICHOLAS (*self-righteously*). What I say is if a man he kills another then he should be killed too.

MAX (*approvingly*). An eye for an eye.

NICHOLAS. And we should use the electric chair. It's no good the hanging.

MAX (*enjoying what he is about to say*). Remember those two they put on the chair in America not long ago, for spying? the bloody thing misfired—ha—they had to do it again. I bet the duty electrician on that job got a rollicking.

FRANK. What do you want them to use—gas ovens?

(MONIQUE *walks past* PETER *to front of stage and waits for him by his station. She has a cup of tea in her hand.* PETER *jumps up and goes to her. They do this every meal-break.*)

PETER. You forgive me?

MONIQUE. I can't keep up a row, I laugh after a while.

PETER. I'm a good boy, really, When's your day off?

MONIQUE. Tomorrow.

PETER. Then I won't see you.

MONIQUE. No.

PETER. What are you going to do?

MONIQUE. In the morning I'm going shopping. In the afternoon I'm going to have my hair done, and in the evening I'm going dancing at the Astra.

PETER. Why do you have to go there? All the prostitutes go there.

MONIQUE. I'm going with Monty.

PETER. Listen Monique. Tell Monty tonight. Ask for a divorce, eh? We can't go on like thieves, we do damage to ourselves, you know that?

MONIQUE. Peter, not here, please. I can't tell him yet.

PETER. Here—inside here (*knocks at his head with his hand*) we do damage. We insult ourselves. I'm not going to wait much longer, you'll see. You think I like this Tivoli?

MONIQUE. Now stop it. Why do you always choose a public place to talk about it? You go on and on, and I keep telling you to give me time. I've promised I will, and I will, so be patient.

PETER. Patient..., me patient?... You don't believe me I won't wait, do you?

MONIQUE. Please yourself.

PETER (*despairingly*). What do you want me to do? Do you want to make me something to laugh at? Three years I'm here now, three. . .

MONIQUE. Oh, ye gods!

(MONIQUE *leaves him.* PETER *is about to become furious but controls himself.*)

PETER (*shouting*). Auf geht's, Irishman. Finish now. Auf geht's.
(KEVIN *takes no notice so* PETER *repeats louder.*)

PETER. Auf geht's, Irishman, auf geht's.

KEVIN. All right, all right.
(PETER *sings his song, lifting* HANS *to his feet.* HANS, KEVIN *and* PETER *return to their stations.*)

CHEF. O.K., Frank.

FRANK. All right, let's get some work done.

CHEF. All right, Michael. Mangolis clear.

MANGOLIS. Sir.
(*All return to their stations.* CHEF *approaches* KEVIN.)

CHEF. You all right?

KEVIN. Yes, Chef.

CHEF. In place and everything?

KEVIN. Yes, Chef.

CHEF. Let me see. (*Watches* KEVIN *start to work.*) All right, but quicker, quicker, quicker.

PETER. Quicker, quicker, quicker, Irishman.

HANS. Quicker, quicker.

PETER. Watch him now the Irishman, soon he won't know what's happening...Hya...Hya, hya. (*He and* HANS *start to sing their song.*)

KEVIN. Does your mother know you're out?
(*The waitresses begin to enter, shouting their orders at the required station. They take plates from hot-plate, cradle them in their arms and order. They appear in greater numbers as the service swings into motion. Queues form in front of first one cook, then another.*)

MOLLY (*to* HANS). Two veal cutlets.

HANS. Two veal cutlets.

GWEN (*to* PETER). Four cod . . . do we order cod?

PETER. Yes, back in five minutes.

WINNIE (*to* PETER). Three turbot.

PETER. Three turbot.

CYNTHIA (*to* HANS). Four veal cutlets.

HANS. Four veal cutlets! Oh baby wait a moment! I...I...I...
    Hast du dir's überlegt? Gehen wir zusammen aus? Ich lade
    dich ein! Wir gehen ins Kino und nachher tanzen. Willst du?

CYNTHIA. No, I—have—to—go—and—get—my—plaice.
    (*said as to someone who doesn't understand a word of English*)

HANS. Oh Gott! My cutlets!

DAPHNE (*to* FRANK). Three legs of chicken.

FRANK. Three legs of chick.

HETTIE (*to* NICHOLAS). Two chicken salad.

NICHOLAS. Two chicken salad.

HANS (*who has been watching* CYNTHIA). Oh my cutlets.

CYNTHIA (*to* KEVIN). Party of eight plaice to begin with.

KEVIN. Eight plaice. She's a worker.

JACKIE (*to* GASTON). Five grilled chops.

GASTON. Five grilled chops.

DAPHNE (*to* NICHOLAS). Three french salad.

HETTIE. I was first.

DAPHNE. Special.

NICHOLAS. Three french salad.

MOLLY (*to* GASTON). Six steaks.

GASTON. Six steaks.

MOLLY (*to* MICHAEL). Four minestrone.

MICHAEL. Four minestrone.

GWEN (*to* FRANK). Two roast chicken and sauté.

FRANK. Two roast chicken and sauté.

CYNTHIA (*to* HANS). These my veal cutlets?

HANS. These are your cutlets! Four Kalbskotletts only for you
    baby!

CYNTHIA. Oh really!

HANS (*to* PETER). Wunderbar! Peter look! Wie die geht! Wie
    die aussieht, die ist genau meine Kragenweite!

PETER (*singing*). 'Falling in love again.'

KEVIN. Hey Peter, any more plaice?

PETER. In the cold cupboard.

   (*In exiting*, KEVIN *knocks into* DAPHNE.)

DAPHNE. Watch it, Irishman.

PETER (*continuing to tease* HANS). 'Falling in love again.'

HANS. Oh Pete, stop it! Ich weiss nicht, was ich anstellen soll! I speak quite good English already.

VIOLET. Four cod.

   (*They obviously don't hear her.*)

HANS. But with her I forget every word.

VIOLET. I said four cod!

HANS (*to* VIOLET). Shut up, baby! (*to* PETER) She is smashing!!

   (VIOLET *goes off.*)

MONIQUE (*to* CHEF). Chef, complaint, minestrone.

PETER (*to* MONIQUE). Now remember, don't forget to remember.

MONIQUE. Remember what?

PETER. What are you doing . . . you don't know what you are doing.

CHEF. Michael, the soup is sour.

MONIQUE (*to* PETER). Your work . . . your work.

   (*While she isn't looking*, MICHAEL *tips the soup straight from one bowl into another, and hands the plate to her.*)

BETTY (*to* ALFREDO). Two roast beef.

ALFREDO. Hold it, hold it.

BETTY. Oh, is it ready?

ALFREDO. Of course it's ready.

PETER. Mangolis, plates!

MANGOLIS. Plates coming up.

GWEN (*to* PETER). Is my four cod ready?

DAPHNE (*to* NICHOLAS). One salad.

WINNIE (*to* FRANK). Two roast pheasant, darling.

FRANK. Oh charming. I love you.

HETTIE (*to* HANS). Two sausages.

JACKIE (*to* ALFREDO). One roast pork.

ALFREDO. One roast pork.

DAPHNE (*to* KEVIN). Two plaice. Oh, where the hell is he?
(*Waits for* KEVIN.)

HETTIE (*to* KEVIN). Three grilled turbot.

JACKIE (*to* PETER). Two cod.

PETER. Two cod.

DAPHNE (*to* KEVIN). Two plaice. Come on, come on Irishman.

KEVIN (*re-entering*). Oh Jesus, Mother of God, and the Holy
Virgin.

GASTON (*who is passing at the same time*). Exo.

DAPHNE (*to* KEVIN). Two plaice.

MOLLY (*to* HANS). My veal cutlets ready?

HANS. What do you think?

HETTIE (*to* KEVIN). Three grilled turbot.

KEVIN. Three grilled turbot.

MOLLY (*to* NICHOLAS). One lobster, one ham salad.

NICHOLAS. One lobster, one ham.

CYNTHIA (*to* MICHAEL). Three omelets au jambon.

MICHAEL. Three jambons.

BETTY (*to* GASTON). Three entrecôte steaks.

GASTON. Three entrecôte steaks.

ANNE (*to* PAUL). My fruit flans ready?

PAUL. I'll bring them up, me old darling.

GWEN (*to* NICHOLAS). Two ham salads.

NICHOLAS. Two ham salads.

GWEN. I want two coffees, Annie love.

ANNE. All right dear.

WINNIE (*to* HANS). Two veal cutlets.

HANS. Two veal cutlets . . . Oh God. Max, veal cutlets and
sausages.

MAX. Yes . . . all right. (*Takes tray which* HANS *throws to him.*)

GASTON. Max, send up steaks and mutton chops quick. (*Almost
hysterical.*)

MAX (*angrily*). Wait a bloody minute will you!

GASTON (*in panic*). I got six steaks ordered already.

MAX. So what am I supposed to do?

GASTON (*to nobody in particular*). Everybody the same in this bloody house. I've always got a big queue before I start. (*Returns mumbling.*)

WINNIE (*to* KEVIN). One plaice please.

KEVIN. One plaice? Right.

BETTY (*to* FRANK). One roast chicken.

FRANK. One roast chicken.

HANS. Come on, Max.

HETTIE (*to* KEVIN). Two grilled salmon, do we order it?

KEVIN. Yes, five minutes. Go on, hop it!

JACKIE (*to* KEVIN). One grilled trout please.

KEVIN (*rushing around*). Right away!

MOLLY (*to* KEVIN). Two plaice please.

KEVIN. All right, all right.

PETER (*shouting while he serves*). Ha-ha! He-he! Ho-ho! They're here! They come!

HETTIE (*to* NICHOLAS). One chicken, one ham salad.

CYNTHIA (*to* PETER). One cod.

PETER. One cod.

WINNIE (*to* MICHAEL). One hamburger.

MICHAEL. One hamburger.

VIOLET. Are my four cod ready?

GWEN (*to* HANS). One veal cutlet.

PETER (*to* VIOLET). When did you order them?

HANS. One veal cutlet.

VIOLET. Five minutes ago. I come past and you were talking to Hans—remember?

PETER. I remember nothing. Come back in five minutes. Next?

VIOLET. You weren't listening, that's what it was.

PETER. You ordered nothing, I say.

MOLLY (*to* MICHAEL). Two minestrone.

PETER. Now come back five minutes' time . . . next.

VIOLET. Well really.

GWEN (*to* PETER). One steamed turbot.

PETER. One steamed turbot.

BETTY (*to* HANS). Three veal cutlets please.

HANS (*mimicking*). Three veal cutlets please.

HEAD WAITER. Violet.

JACKIE (*to* NICHOLAS). Two ham, one lobster salad.

DAPHNE (*to* ANNE). Three fruit flan.

HANS (*to* BETTY, *who has waited*). What's the matter with you . . . you can't see the cutlets cook.

BETTY. Well, last time I waited.

HANS. Well, last time I waited.

BETTY. Oh get lost . . . excuse me Harry. (*to* HEAD WAITER, *who is passing*)

WINNIE (*to* GASTON). Three steaks.

HEAD WAITER (*to* CHEF). Ten minutes ago, Violet ordered four cod. They're not ready yet.

  (KEVIN, GASTON *and* MICHAEL *call for plates.*)

CHEF. Peter . . . the cod not ready yet?

PETER. She's a liar that one, she ordered nothing.

CHEF. Come on, come on.

PETER. One cod, two cod.

DAPHNE (*to* ANNE). Two coffees.

PETER. Three cod, four cod.

  (*As* VIOLET *turns with the plates,* MANGOLIS, *who is passing knocks her, and the plates fall to the ground.*)

JACKIE (*to* ANNE). Three coffees.

VIOLET. Oh God, God, God, I can't, I can't.

GWEN. Don't upset yourself, love.

VIOLET. Look at it all, I can't work like this. I'm not used to this way of working.

BETTY (*to* MICHAEL). One minestrone.

VIOLET. I've never worked like this before, never, never.

  (*During this the* CHEF *calls* FRANK, *who calls* MANGOLIS *to clear the broken china.*)

PETER. Too old, too old my sweetheart. Go home old woman —for the young this work—go home.

HANS (*to* PETER). Oh stop it, shut up.

(PETER *makes a face after* CHEF *and when it is safe he begins to sing his song while working. Half way through, he breaks off and rushes to oven. There is something vast and Shakespearian in the way* PETER *moves—he is always wanting to play the fool.*)

GWEN (*to* HANS). One veal cutlet.

PETER (*to* KEVIN). Oh God! She burns! The cod! Hya, hya, hya. She burns, Irishman. No good, no good. (*Rushes the frying-pan with the burnt fish to the dustbin nearby, and covers it with paper.*) Ssh, ssssh. Hya, hya, hya.

HANS (*to* PETER, *loudly in the midst of his own work*). That is not too good work Peter, not good work mein Lieber. Pig's work. (*Laughs and points to* KEVIN, *who has large queue at his station.*) We have busy time, Irishman, yes?

KEVIN. Bloody comedian.

HETTIE (*to* KEVIN). My salmon ready?

KEVIN. Your what?

HETTIE. Me grilled salmon.

KEVIN. How many do you want?

HETTIE. Two.

CYNTHIA (*to* MICHAEL). My three omelets.

MICHAEL. Your three omelets.

DAPHNE (*to* KEVIN). Two salmon.

JACKIE (*to* KEVIN). Three sardines.

KEVIN. Peter, for God's sake will you give me a hand?

HETTIE (*to* MICHAEL). Two veg soups.

PETER (*helping* KEVIN). Let's go Irishman, let's go. The next.

DAPHNE. Two salmon.

PETER. Right.

BETTY (*to* HANS). My veal cutlets.

HANS. Your veal cutlets.

PETER. And the next?

JACKIE (*to* PETER). Three sardines.

BETTY (*to* HANS). Oh come on, lobster-face.

HANS. What does it mean, lobster-face?

PETER. And the next?

WINNIE (*to* PETER). Three plaice.

HANS (*to* BETTY). Ein, zwei, drei.

PETER (*to* WINNIE). One, two, three.

BETTY (*to* PETER). Two plaice.

> (*While* PETER *has been helping* KEVIN, *the following three orders pile up on his unattended station.*)

MOLLY. One turbot.

GWEN. One steamed halibut.

CYNTHIA. Two cod.

MOLLY. Oh come on, Peter.

> (PETER *rushes to his station, laughing like a merry fool going into battle.*)

PETER. Look at this—hya, hya—good morning ladies—and the next . . .

MOLLY (*to* PETER). One turbot. (PETER *serves her, and cries out* 'Next, next,' *and so on.*)

GWEN (*to* PETER). One steamed halibut.

JACKIE (*to* FRANK). Three legs of chicken.

FRANK. Three chicken.

KEVIN (*to* PETER). I've run out of lemons!

PETER (*with rude indifference*). Well cut some more then. The next?

KEVIN. Let me borrow your cutting-board then, please. (*He moves to take it from* PETER's *bench.*)

PETER (*stops his work, and jumping on* KEVIN, *grabs board: in the kitchen it is every man for himself now*). Oh no, no, no, no my friend. The plate-room, the plate-room, in the plate-room, you'll find them. This is mine, I have need of it.

KEVIN. But I'll give it back in a few seconds.

PETER (*pointing*). The plate-room. (*Slams his hand down on the board for emphasis; to a waitress—*) What do you want?

KEVIN (*going to plate-room*). Well, speak a little human like will yer please?

PETER. No time, no time. Next.

CYNTHIA (*to* PETER). Two cod.

JACKIE (*to* NICHOLAS). One cheese salad.

VIOLET (*to* NICHOLAS). One ham salad. (*tearfully*)

BETTY (*to* GASTON). My steaks ready yet?

VIOLET (*to* ANNE). A fruit flan and two coffees.

GASTON (*to* BETTY). About time.

BETTY. I'm sorry.

DAPHNE (*to* FRANK). Two roast chicken.

FRANK. Two roast chicken.

WINNIE (*to* ALFREDO). Two roast veal and spaghetti.

JACKIE (*to* MICHAEL). One prawn omelet.

MICHAEL. One prawn.

GWEN (*to* ALFREDO). Two roast beef.

ALFREDO. Two roast beef.

MOLLY (*to* KEVIN). Two sole.

CYNTHIA (*to* KEVIN). Three plaice.

DAPHNE (*to* GASTON). Two lamb chops.

HETTIE (*to* MICHAEL). Two minestrones.

MONIQUE (*to* PETER). Four cod.

PETER. What?

MONIQUE. Violet's four cod.

MOLLY (*about* KEVIN). He's never here, this one.

PETER (*to* MONIQUE). You wait for me afterwards.

MONIQUE. I'll wait for you.

CYNTHIA (*to* KEVIN). Come on Irishman, my plaice.

BETTY (*to* MICHAEL). One minestrone.

PETER (*to* MONIQUE). We go for a stroll?

MONIQUE. Yes, we go for a stroll.

MOLLY (*to* CYNTHIA). We'll lose all those tips.

GWEN (*to* HANS). Four veal cutlets.

HANS. Four veal cutlets.

MOLLY (*to* KEVIN). Me sole, luvvy, where's me sole?

KEVIN (*re-entering*). Wait a bloody minute, can't you.

MOLLY (*to* KEVIN). Two.

GWEN (*to* PETER). Two halibut.

BETTY (*to* MICHAEL). Three hamburgers.

CYNTHIA (*to* KEVIN). Three plaice. There's no time for breathing here, you know.

KEVIN. Jesus is this a bloody madhouse.

MICHAEL. Three hamburgers.

NICHOLAS. Plates.

MANGOLIS. Plates.

KEVIN. Have you all gone barking-raving-bloody-mad.

> (*At this point all the waitresses have got into a continuous circle of orders round and round the kitchen, as the volume of the ovens increases and the lights slowly fade to blackout. The calls of orders and for plates and more meat, etc., continue through the blackness until the stage is clear and ready for the interlude. The author would prefer there to be no interval at this point but recognizes the wish of theatre bars to make some money.*)

PETER'S SONG

Hi lee hi lo hi la   Hi lee hi lo hi la   hi lee

hi lo   hi la ha ha ha ha ha   *continue down the scale in laughter*

hya hya hya hya.

INTERLUDE

Lights fade up on the sound of a guitar.

It is afternoon break. The sounds of the oven are at half. PAUL *and* RAYMOND *are working in their corner. These are the only two who stay through the afternoon.* KEVIN *is flat out on his back on a wooden bench, exhausted.* DIMITRI *is slowly sweeping up.* PETER *is sitting by a table waiting for* MONIQUE. HANS *is in a corner with a guitar, singing 'Ah sinner-man' in German.*

KEVIN. Finished! I'm done! I'm boiled! You can serve me up for supper!

PAUL (*as if ordering a meal*). Two portions of boiled Irishman please! With garnish!

RAYMOND (*also calling*). Two fried tomatoes on his ears, potatoes round his head, and stuff his mouth with an extra helping of peas.

KEVIN. I'll produce me own gravy! But did you see it? Did-you-see-that? Fifteen hundred customers, an' half of them eating fish. *I* had to start work on a Friday!

RAYMOND. It's every day the same, my friend.

KEVIN (*raising himself up*). Look at me. I'm soaking. Look at this jacket. I can wring it out. That's not sweat, no man carries that much water. (*flopping back again*) Kevin, you'll drop dead if you stay. I'm warning you Kevin, take a tip from a friend, hop it! Get out! You've got your youth Kevin, keep it! This is no place for a human being—you'll drop dead, I'm telling yous.

DIMITRI. Hey Irishman, what you grumbling about this place for? Is different anywhere else? People come and people go, bit excitement, big noise. (*Makes noise and gesticulates.*) What for? In the end who do you know? You make a friend, you going to be all you life his friend but when you go from here—pshtt! You forget! Why you grumble about this one kitchen?

PETER. You're a very intelligent boy, Dimitri.

DIMITRI. And you're a bloody fool. I'm not sure I want to talk with you.

KEVIN. Oh not the Gaston row again. All the morning I hear how Peter give Gaston a black eye. It's the break, no rows please, it's peace. Can you hear it? It's lovely, it's silence. It's nothing—ahhh! (*Moves.*) Oooh—I'm drowning, in my own sweat. Christ! What a way to die.

DIMITRI (*to* PETER). A bloody fool you!

> (PETER *picks up a cardboard box, and puts it over* DIMITRI's *head.* DIMITRI *flings it off angrily and is about to throw it back, but he sees* PETER *with his head in his hands. Instead, he takes out a cigarette box, and begins rolling* PETER *a cigarette. He gives the paper to* PETER *to lick, then continues folding it, and hands it to him.*)

PETER. Hey Irishman, I thought you didn't like this place. Why don't you go home and sleep.

KEVIN. Me home is a room and a bed and a painting of the Holy Virgin. It'll always be there.

PETER. Like this place, this house—this too, it'll always be here. That's a thought for you Irishman. This—this madhouse it's always here. When you go, when I go, when Dimitri go—this kitchen stays. It'll go on when we die, think about that. We work here—eight hours a day, and yet—it's nothing. We take nothing. Here—the kitchen, here—you. You and the kitchen. And the kitchen don't mean nothing to you and you don't mean to the kitchen nothing. Dimitri is right you know—why do you grumble about this kitchen? What about the offices and the factories? There Irishman—what do you say to that?

KEVIN. You want come in one morning and find it gone?

PETER. Just one morning. Imagine it, eh? Gone. All this gone.

KEVIN. So you'd be out of work!

PETER. So I'd die?

KEVIN. It doesn't worry you I suppose.

HANS. Du träumst schon wieder.

KEVIN. What's he say?

PETER. He say—I'm dreaming.

> (PETER *stands up, and begins idly strolling round the kitchen. Picks up dustbin-lid, a long ladle—shield and sword —lunges at* RAYMOND. RAYMOND *picks up a whisk. A few seconds' duel.* PETER *raises his arms in surrender.*)

PETER. Yah! War! Did you used to play like this, at war, with dustbin-lids and things? I did. Yah! Not very good, eh Irishman? War? Kids playing at war grow up peaceful they say, I think not so simple, eh? Me I never liked war games. I had my own group—boys, we'd build things. Castles, huts, camps.

> (*During this,* PETER *has taken two dustbins, puts one on the corner of the stove and one on the opposite corner of his hot-plate. He then puts a tall container on top of each and saucepans on top of these. Next he puts* DIMITRI'*s broom across the top, and hangs dish-cloths on the handles. He then notices a vase of flowers on the Chef's table, and, selecting the largest, he gives the remainder to* PAUL; *he puts his flower through one of the saucepan handles. With his back to the audience, he faces his creation.*)

PAUL. Beautiful, what is it?

PETER. It's my arch, and I was ... And I was ... (*grabbing a long ladle to use as a saluting sword*) I was ein grosser Deutscher Ritter!

HANS. Hey Peter—weisst du noch?

> (*At this point* HANS *starts to play the Horst Wessel song on the guitar.* PETER *does the goose-step through his arch while* PAUL *throws flowers over him and* HANS.)

KEVIN (*sings*). And the Irish Republican Army made muck of the whole bloody lot. Now isn't that something mad, now.

PETER. You think this is madness?

KEVIN. Well, isn't it? Isn't it kids playing and all that carry-on?

PETER. This one says games and that one says dreams. You think it's a waste of time? You know what a game is? A dream? It's the time when you forget what you are and you make what you could be. When a man dreams—he grows, big, better. You find that silly?

HANS. Du bist zu alt, Peter!

PETER. I'm *not* too old, never, never too old, don't tell me that. Too old! When you're dead you're too old.

HANS. Aha, und du glaubst wir haben hier Zeit zum träumen.

PETER. There is! There is time to dream. I want to dream. Everyone should dream, once in a life everyone should dream. Hey Irishman, you dream, how do you dream, tell us?

KEVIN. You play our own games, Peter, leave me out of it, I'm past it.

PETER. You know when a man is not a man? When he's ashamed of being a child. That's you Irishman. You're ashamed of being a child. Why you ashamed? We all friends here, why you ashamed to dream, I give you the chance.

KEVIN. I'm obliged!

PETER. Hey Paul, Raymondo, Dimitri, stop work a minute. You got time. Here, come here. We are all given a chance to dream. No one is going to laugh, we love each other, we protect each other—someone tell us a dream, just to us, no one else, the ovens are low, the customers gone, Marango is gone, it's all quiet. God has given us a chance now, we never have the opportunity again, so dream—someone— who? Dimitri—you, you dream first.

DIMITRI. In this place? With iron around me? And dustbins? And black walls?

PETER. Pretend! There's no dustbins, that's a big beautiful arch there. Pretend! The walls are skies, yes? The iron, it's rock on a coast; the tables, (*thinks*) they're rose bushes; and the ovens are the noise of the winds. Look at the lights— stars, Dimitri.

HANS. Peter, du verschwendest deine Zeit!

PETER. So what! So what if I waste time? It's good to be able to waste time. I got another sixty years to live, I can afford it. Dimitri—dream—a little dream, what you see?

DIMITRI. A little, a little er—what you call it—a small house, sort of—

PAUL. A hut?

DIMITRI. No—

KEVIN. A shed?

DIMITRI. That's right, a shed. With instruments, and tools, and I make lots of radios and television sets maybe, and . . .

PETER. Ach no, silly boy. That's a hobby, that's not what you really want. You want more, more, Dimitri—

DIMITRI. I—I—I can't, Peter, I can't see more, I try but I can't see more.

PETER. Poor Dimitri—hey Irishman, you—you dream.

KEVIN. If you think because I'm Irish I'm going to start prattling on about goblins and leprechauns you've got another think coming—

PETER. No, no, not fairies, a real dream, about men—

KEVIN. But I don't dream of men—

PETER. What then?

KEVIN. Sleep! Sleep me. Most people sleep and dream; me—I dream of sleep!

PETER. What is it with you all? Hans—you, what are your dreams?

(HANS *sings on, as though not answering the question. Then—*)

HANS. Money! Geld, Peter, Geld! With money I'm a good man! I'm generous! I love all the world! Money, Pete! Money! Money! Money! (*Continues singing.*)

PETER. How can you talk of money, Hans, when you're singing?

HANS. Dreaming, mein Lieber, dreaming, dreaming.

PETER. Raymondo?

RAYMOND. Me? Women!

PETER. Which women? Large, small? Happy? Black? Yellow? What kind?

RAYMOND. There *is* more than one kind?

PETER. Raymond—you make me very sad. Paul—you.

PAUL. Do me a favour.

PETER. Please!

PAUL. No. (*Relents*) Listen, Peter . . . I'll tell you something. I'm going to be honest with you. You don't mind if I'm honest? Right! I'm going to be honest with you. I don't like you. Now wait a minute, let me finish. I don't like you! I think you're a pig! You bully, you're jealous, you go mad with your work, you always quarrel. All right! But now it's quiet, the ovens are low, the work has stopped for a little and now I'm getting to know you. I still think you're a pig— only now, not so much of a pig. So that's what I dream. I dream of a friend. You give me a rest, you give me silence, you take away this mad kitchen so I make friends, so I think —maybe all the people I thought were pigs are not so much pigs.

PETER. You think people are pigs, eh?

PAUL. Listen, I'll tell you something. I agree with Dimitri also; when the world is filled with kitchens you get pigs—I'll tell you. Next door to me, next door where I live is a bus driver. Comes from Hoxton, he's my age, married and got two kids. He says good morning to me, I ask him how he is, I give his children sweets. That's our relationship. Somehow he seems frightened to say too much, you know? God forbid I might ask him for something. So we make no demands on each other. Then one day the busmen go on strike. He's out for five weeks. Every morning I say to him 'Keep going mate, you'll win.' Every morning I give him words of encouragement; I say I understand his cause. I've got to get up earlier to get to work but I don't mind. We're neigh-bours. We're workers together, he's pleased. Then, one

Sunday, there's a peace march. I don't believe they do much good but I go, because in this world a man's got to show he can have his say. The next morning he comes up to me and he says, now listen to this, he says 'Did you go on that peace march yesterday?' So I says Yes, I did go on that peace march yesterday. So then he turns round to me and he says, 'You know what? A bomb should have been dropped on the lot of them! It's a pity,' he says, 'that they had children with them cos a bomb should've been dropped on the lot!' And you know what was upsetting him? The march was holding up the traffic, the buses couldn't move so fast! Now I don't want him to say I'm right, I don't want him to agree with what I did, but what terrifies me is that he didn't stop to think that this man helped me in my cause so maybe, only *maybe*, there's something in his cause. I'll talk about it. No! The buses were held up so drop a bomb he says, on the lot! And you should've seen the hate in his eyes, as if I'd murdered his child. Like an animal he looked. And the horror is this—that there's a wall, a big wall between me and millions of people like him. And I think—where will it end? What do you do about it? And I look around me, at the kitchen, at the factories, at the enormous bloody buildings going up with all those offices and all those people in them, and I think, Christ! I think, Christ, Christ, Christ! I agree with you Peter—maybe one morning we should wake up and find them all gone. But then I think: I should stop making pastries? The factory worker should stop making trains and cars? The miner should leave the coals where it is? (*Pause.*) *You* give *me* an answer. You give me your dream.

KEVIN. Hush pâtissier! Hush! It's quiet now. Gently now.

(HANS *throws one of the red flowers to* PAUL. *There is a long silence.* HANS, *who had stopped playing, now continues. The ovens hum.* PAUL *sticks the flower in his lapel.*)

PETER. I ask for dreams—you give me nightmares.

PAUL. So I've dreamt! Is it my fault if it's a nightmare?

KEVIN. We're waiting for your dream now, Peter boy.

DIMITRI (*jumping up suddenly*). This is the United Nations, eh? A big conference. Is Russia here, and America and France and England—and Germany too. Is all here. And they got on a competition. Is finished the wars, is finished the rows. Everybody gone home. We got time on our hands. A prize of one million dollars for the best dream. Raymondo he want a new woman every night. I want a workshop. Paul he wants a friend. Irishman he wants a bed and Hans he just want the million dollars. Big opportunity! Come on Peter, a big dream.

PETER (*looking around*). All this gone?

DIMITRI. You said so. One morning you come here, to this street here, and the kitchen is gone. And you look around for more kitchens and is none anywhere. What you want to do? The United Nations wants to know.

PAUL. Come on, come on!

PETER. Shush, shush!

(PETER *suddenly confronted with his own idea becomes embarrassed and shy. He laughs.*)

PETER. I can't. I can't.

(MONIQUE *arrives and* PETER *forgets everything and becomes the all-consumed lover, the excited child.*)

MONIQUE. Ready?

PETER. Finished? I come I come. Hey Irishman, you'll soon be coming back. Go home. Change. You catch pneumonia. (*excitedly*) Auf geht's, auf geht's!

(*The mad* PETER *rushes out with his* MONIQUE. *The rest are left. The guitar and the hum of the ovens.*)

DIMITRI (*shouting at the absent Peter*). Fool! Bloody fool! We wait for a dream.

PAUL. I don't know what you see in him.

DIMITRI. I don't know what I see in him either. Bloody fool!

KEVIN. Bloody volcano if you ask me. I'm away. (*Rises.*)

PAUL (*returning to his work*). He hasn't got a dream.

KEVIN. It's all mad talk if you ask me. I don't see no point in it. I don't see no point in that Peter bloke either. He talks about peace and dreams and when I ask him if I could use his cutting-board to cut me lemons on this morning he told me—get your own. Dreams? See yous!

(KEVIN *exits.* HANS *is still playing.* DIMITRI *returns to his sweeping.*)

PAUL (*to* DIMITRI). So *you* tell me the point of all that. I don't even know what I was saying myself.

DIMITRI. Why should I know? Sometimes things happen and no one sees the point—and then suddenly, something else happen and you see the point. Peter not a fool! You not a fool! People's brain moves all the time. *All* the time. I'm telling you.

(DIMITRI *sweeps on.* HANS *finishes his song, rises, bows, slings his guitar and exits.*

This next scene happens very, very slowly to denote the passing of the afternoon.)

PAUL. Best part of the day.

RAYMOND. When they're gone I slow down.

PAUL (*throwing a cigarette end to* DIMITRI). Here's another bit of debris for you. Longest part of the day though isn't it?

RAYMOND (*offering to* PAUL *from Nicholas's table*). Tomato? Carrot? Cucumber? (PAUL *declines all.*) Yes, the longest part.

(*Enter* MANGOLIS. DIMITRI *strikes the bench and table and part of the arch. The afternoon is over.* MANGOLIS *is singing a Greek air;* GASTON *enters followed by* NICHOLAS, *and the four of them gradually start a Greek dance....*)

PART TWO

. . . At the end of the Greek dance, DIMITRI *starts to kick a cardboard box, as in football;* MICHAEL *entering intercepts it.*

MICHAEL. And that great little inside left, Michael Dawson, has the ball again. Will he miss this golden opportunity? Can he hold his own against the great Arsenal backs? He *does!* Yes! Past Wills, past MacCullough, past Young and he's going to shoot, he *shoots!*—and it's a goal, a goal, yes, his fifth goal, making the score Leyton Orient eighteen, Arsenil nil. What a game! What a boy! Look at this place, like a battlefield, grrr—it smells of the dead.

(MONIQUE *enters, slamming the door, and exits into the dining-room, in a furious temper.*)

PAUL. Well, they started the afternoon happy. Did you have a good afternoon, Michael?

MICHAEL. Too bloody good . . . St. James Park. Lying in the sun. Dozing. The girls—aaaah! Hey, I saw Nick and Daphne in the park.

PAUL. There's nice for you.

MICHAEL. Rowing on the lake.

RAYMOND. How touching. Aaaaaah!

MICHAEL. He wasn't doing the row though! You boys are lucky, not having to break in the afternoon, come back to work.

PAUL. I thought you liked the place.

MICHAEL. I don't mind the coming in, it's the coming back. Not old Alfred though. Look at him—in, out, cook, serve— he doesn't mind.

(ALFREDO *has entered and gone straight to his work. Following him is* PETER, *who hangs back.*)

ALFREDO. Well come on Peter boy, work, it won't hurt you. Come on then, stock up, replenish, boy.

PETER. My arch—where is it? Who took it down, who took my arch away? Let it stay—let Marango see it.

(GASTON *is emptying waste into one dustbin.*)

PETER (*to* GASTON). You leave it! You leave it!

(ALFREDO *approaches him. During this conversation the others enter.*)

ALFREDO. You are not ill, are you?

PETER. Who knows.

ALFREDO. No pain nor nothing?

PETER. No. Alfredo, look—

ALFREDO. Good! You have all your teeth?

PETER. Yes.

ALFREDO. Good! You have good lodgings?

PETER. Yes.

ALFREDO. So tell me what you're unhappy for.

PETER. Alfredo, you are a good cook, uh? You come in the morning, you go straight to work, you ask nobody anything, you tell nobody anything. You are ready to start work before we are, you never panic. Tell me, is this a good house?

ALFREDO (*drily*). Depends. It's not bad for Mr. Marango, you know.

MICHAEL (*approaching* PETER). Peter, give me a cigarette please! (PETER *does so.* MICHAEL *stays on to listen.*)

ALFREDO. I'm an old man. It's finished for me. Mind you I've worked in places where I could do good cooking. But it doesn't matter now. Now I work only for the money.

MICHAEL. Quite right! A match Peter please.

PETER (*to* MICHAEL, *looking for matches*). You like it here, don't you?

MICHAEL. The ovens—

PETER. No, I got no matches.

MICHAEL. I love the sound of the ovens. Nick, got a light?

(NICHOLAS *throws him matches.*)

PETER. Idiot! He loves the sound of the ovens! You stand before them all day! They're red hot! You fry first a bit of ham and an egg in a tin; then someone orders an onion soup and you put soup and bread and cheese in another tin, and you grill that; then someone orders an omelet and you rush to do that; then someone throws you a hamburger and you fry that. You go up you go down you jump here you jump there, you sweat till steam comes off your back.

MICHAEL (*moving across to* NICHOLAS *for a light*). I love it.

PETER (*returning head to arms*). Good luck to you.

ALFREDO (*to* MONIQUE). Here, you talk to him—he's your generation. (*Moves off.*)

PAUL (*to* RAYMOND). Come on Lightning, let's get some work done.

MONIQUE (*to* PETER). Are you still sulking? It was your fault we rowed, not mine, you're just like a little boy.

(*The* CHEF *and* FRANK *enter. The* CHEF *breaks between* PETER *and* MONIQUE.)

PETER. Would you like me old and fat, like your husband? Then you'd have to find a new lover! I sympathize with Monty sometimes.

MONIQUE. You feel sorry for him?

PETER. Would you like me to hate him? I can't! I try but I can't, it would be easier but I can't. A good man, kind and no vices—who can hate such persons?

MONIQUE. I'm sorry I left you standing in the street.

PETER. You're always sorry afterwards, like a dog she leaves me.

MONIQUE. Where did you go?

PETER. Never mind—I went. Go on, go. Go wipe your glasses, it's nearly time. Go, leave me.

MONIQUE. Look at you. Look at you . . . is it any wonder I don't know where the hell I am . . . you behave like this. I come to apologize, I say I'm sorry, I speak reasonably and now you . . . you . . . (*Exits.*)

MAX (*to* NICHOLAS). What did you marry her for then?

NICHOLAS. Because I love her, that's why. Ha— (*digs* FRANK) did you hear that? Why did I marry her, because I love her. And you?

MAX (*also digging* FRANK). Because she told me I was big for my age. Hey, did you read about the man who took a young girl into his house, his wife was there, and they all sat undressed watching television. His wife was there! With him! All undressed! Watching television!

FRANK (*drily*). So what happened? They caught cold? (*to* KEVIN). Hey, this isn't a rest room, get on with your work.

(*Enter* DAPHNE *and* HETTIE, *giving out new menus.*)

KEVIN. I'll be taking *my* leave tonight by Christ.

GASTON. You'll get used to it. It's good money.

(*Enter* VIOLET *chatting with* ANNE, *followed by* HEAD WAITER, *who goes to* CHEF'S *table.*)

KEVIN. To hell with the money an' all. I like me pay but not for this. It's too big here, man, it's high pressure all the time. An' the food! Look at the food! I never cooked so bad since I was in the army. An' no one is after caring much either!

VIOLET. And what about the waitresses, we're the animals, everybody pushing everybody else out of the way.

HEAD WAITER. Never mind, Violet. You got over your first morning all right. This evening won't be so bad, nobody will push you. It'll just be hot—hot and close—for everyone.

VIOLET. I can remember working in places where you had to move like a ballet dancer, weave in and out of tables with grace. There was room, it was civilized.

KEVIN. Starch and clean finger-nails—I heard about it.

(HETTIE *goes off sniggering at* VIOLET.)

VIOLET (*to* HETTIE). And we didn't mind either—we had to queue up and be inspected, all of us, chefs too—it was civilized. I once served the Prince of Wales. Look at me, bruises.

KEVIN. Look at her! Look at me, three stone lighter!

HANS (*to* KEVIN). Marango will try to make you stay.

KEVIN. Now there's a man. Have you watched him? One of the girls dropped some cups by there this morning and he cried, 'me wages' he cried. 'All me wages down there!' And do take notice of the way he strolls among us all? I thought he'd a kind face, but when he's done talking with you his kindness evaporates. In thin air it goes, sudden, and his face gets worried as though today were the last day and he had to be closing for good and he were taking a last sad glance at everything going on. This mornin' he watched me a while, and then walked away shaking his head as though I were dying and there was not a drop of hope for me left an' all.

HANS (*to* PETER). What he has said?

PETER. Marango spielt den lieben Gott!

(DAPHNE *wanders away but not before she takes a piece of cake from* PAUL.)

PAUL (*to* DAPHNE). Bon appetit.

GASTON. Paul you got some cake?

PAUL (*to* RAYMOND). Give the boy some cake. (*to* HANS) You got over this morning yet?

HANS (*taking a cake* RAYMOND *is offering round*). This morning, ach! He's a big fool, that Max. He's like a dustbin.

RAYMOND. So why you take notice? Look at them.

(MAX *and* NICHOLAS *are pointing at each other in some sort of argument, waving fingers, pulling faces and swaying.*)

NICHOLAS. No! No! No! I'm never going to listen to you again, never.

MAX. Good, very good. I'm fed up with you hanging around me anyway. 'Max should I do this, Max should I do that?' Well, Max isn't your father.

NICHOLAS. You're damn right he's not my father. My father was a man with kindness, my father never betray what I tell him.

MAX. Well *I* didn't betray what you told me either, I keep telling you—

NICHOLAS. My father brought up nine children and all of them good people—

MAX. I didn't tell anyone, I keep telling you—

NICHOLAS. My father—

MAX. Your father nothing! He's been dead since you was three years old so give that one a miss also.

RAYMOND. The first thing in the morning they come in and drink a bottle of beer. Then they're happy. All day they drink.

PAUL (*to* HANS). What did Max say then exactly?

HANS. He doesn't like I talk in German. (*tragically*) You know Paul you—you are a Jew and me—I'm German; we suffer together.

(PAUL *stiffens, relaxes, laughs ironically, hands* HANS *the red flower from his lapel.* HANS *returns to his station.*)

KEVIN (*to* HANS). Is that a Jew then?

HANS (*sentimentally*). A very good boy.

KEVIN. Well who'd have thought that, now.

(*At this point a* TRAMP *wanders into the kitchen. He is looking for the* CHEF. *Everyone stares at him and grins.*)

MAX (*shouting across to* BERTHA). Bertha, ha, ha, is this your old man come after you? (*General laughter.*)

BERTHA. I'll come after you in a minute, pack it in.

(*The* TRAMP *comes over to the group of young men and talks to* KEVIN.)

TRAMP. 'Scuse me. The Chef please, which'n is he?

KEVIN. Napoleon there.

TRAMP. 'Scuse me, Chef (*touching his knee*), war disabled, I don't usually ask for food but I lost me pensions book see? I don't like to ask but . . .

CHEF. Michael, clean a tin and give him some soup.

TRAMP (*to* KEVIN). Don't usually do this. Can't do anything till they trace me book. (*to* HANS) Got it in the desert, 'gainst Rommel.

HANS. Rommel! Aha!

TRAMP. Got papers to prove it too. Here, look, papers! Always carry these around with me, everyone got to have his papers and I always carry mine. Be daft for the like o' me to leave them anywhere, wouldn't it? Who'd believe me otherwise, see? Papers! Whatcha making? Spaghetti bolonaizeeee? That's good that Italian food. Do you put bay leaves in? Good with bay leaves, not the same without. Bay leaves, red peppers, all that stuff. What's this? (*Sees half-made arch.*) A castle? (*Sees dish-cloth, picks it up, and idly balances it on the tip of one of the handles, laughs and looks to see whether others are amused.* MICHAEL *hands him a tin of soup.*)

MICHAEL. Here you are.

TRAMP. Got a cigarette?

MICHAEL. Yes, and I'm smoking it.

MAX. Go on, 'op it, be quick, we got work.

PETER (*goes up to* TRAMP, *and looks in the tin; takes tin from* TRAMP *and offers it to* MAX). You drink it?

MAX. Ah get out of it, you and your high and bloody mighty gestures. *I* work for my living. Fool!

(PETER *ignores him and tosses the tin into the dustbin. Then he moves to* HANS' *station, and brings back two meat cutlets which he gives to the* TRAMP.)

PETER. Take these cutlets. (*gently pushing him*) Now go, quick, whist!

(*But he is not quick enough. The* CHEF *approaches, and stands looking on.*)

CHEF (*quietly*). What's that?

PETER. I gave him some cutlets.

CHEF. Mr. Marango told you to give him?

PETER. No, but . . .

CHEF. You heard me say, perhaps?

PETER. No, I . . .

CHEF. You have authority suddenly?

PETER (*impatiently*). So what's a couple of cutlets, we going bankrupt or something?

CHEF. It's four and six that's what, and it's me who's Chef that's what and . . . (PETER *moves away muttering* 'ach'. *The* CHEF *follows him, annoyed now.*) Don't think we're too busy

I can't sack you. Three years is nothing you know, you don't buy the place in three years, you hear me? You got that? Don't go thinking I won't sack you.

(*By this time* MR. MARANGO *appears on his round, hands in pocket.*)

MARANGO. Yes?

CHEF. The tramp—Peter gave him a cutlet, it was his own supper.

(CHEF *returns to his work, dispersing the crowd on the way.* MR. MARANGO *simply nods his head at* PETER. *It is a sad nodding, as though* PETER *had just insulted him. He walks from right of stage to the left in a half circle round* PETER, *nodding his head all the time.*)

MARANGO (*softly*). Sabotage. (*Pause.*) It's sabotage you do to me. (*sadly taking his right hand out of his pocket, and waving it round the kitchen*) It's my fortune here and you give it away. (*He moves off muttering* 'sabotage'.)

PETER. But it . . .

MARANGO (*not even bothering to look round*). Yes, yes, I'm always wrong—of course—yes, yes. (*Moves off into dining-room.*)

(*Everyone settles back into place.* PETER *goes to get a cup of coffee and makes faces at Marango's back, then he returns beside* ALFREDO. HANS *joins them.*)

HANS. Ou, pass auf, der ist wirklich hinter dir her!

PETER. Ach, er erwartet, dass die ganze Welt auf seine Küche aufpasst!

KEVIN. I seem to remember being told not to grumble by someone.

PETER. A bastard man. A bastard house.

KEVIN. And he also said you could get used to anything.

PETER. But this house is like—is like—

PAUL. Yeah? What is it like?

PETER. God in heaven, I don't know what it's like. If only it—if only it—

KEVIN. Yes, yes, we know all that—if only it would all go.

PETER. Just one morning—to find it gone.

PAUL. Fat lot of good you'd be if it went—you couldn't even cough up a dream when it was necessary.

PETER. A dream?

HANS. Ja, Pete, wo bleibt der Traum, den du uns versprochen hast?

PETER. I can't, I can't. (*sadly*) I can't dream in a kitchen! (*Violently kicks down other half of arch.*)

HANS. Aha! Und jetzt spielst du wieder den wilden Mann! (*Enter* BERTHA *with a colander and* MONIQUE. *Both watch this.*)

BERTHA (*to* MONIQUE). Why don't you hop it, out of here, girl like you—

MONIQUE. Girl like me *what*?

BERTHA. Pack it in, Monique. Peter I mean—dissolve it.

MONIQUE. Just like that?

BERTHA. Just like that.

MONIQUE. Just—like—that, huh! Twice he's given me a baby, twice I've disappointed him. He wanted them both. Dissolve that.

BERTHA. Aaaaah why don't we all hop it?

MONIQUE. Good question, Aunty Bertha.

PETER (*moving to* MONIQUE). I'm sorry.

MONIQUE. Not an attractive future, is it? Apologizing backwards and forwards. First you, then me . . .

PETER. Did you see that tramp?

MONIQUE. What tramp?

PETER. You didn't hear?

MONIQUE. Hear what?

PETER (*boasting and laughing, trying to pacify her*). I had a row about him, Mr. Marango and the Chef there, they wanted to give him a dirty tin full of soup so I threw it away and gave him some cutlets.

MONIQUE. And Marango caught you?

PETER (*imitating*). 'Sabotage,' the old man said. 'Sabotage, all my fortune you take away.'

MONIQUE. Oh Peter!

PETER (*tenderly*). Listen, do you want to know where I went this afternoon? To buy your birthday present.

MONIQUE. A present?

WINNIE (*to* HANS). One veal cutlet.

WINNIE (*to* KEVIN). Two plaice.

> (PETER *takes out a necklace, and places it round her neck. She relents, turns to him, and pulls him to her, bites his neck.*)

CYNTHIA (*to* HANS). One veal cutlet.

HANS. One veal cutlet. (*long sad glance at her*)

CYNTHIA (*to* MICHAEL). One minestrone.

MICHAEL. One minestrone.

GWEN (*to* MICHAEL). Minestrone.

PETER. Ah, you want to eat me. How do you want me? Grilled? Fried? Underdone? Well done?

> (*While* PETER *and* MONIQUE *continue to talk affectionately, a sudden cry comes up from the back of the kitchen.* WINNIE *has doubled up in pain, and passed out. A crowd rushes to her—it all happens very quickly, hardly noticed. The boys at the table simply glance round and watch but do not move.* PETER *and* MONIQUE *do not even hear it. We can only hear a few confused voices.*)

ALFREDO. All right, now don't crowd round, take her into the dining-room. Don't crowd round. (*Crowd disperses as* WINNIE *is taken into dining-room.*)

PAUL. Who was it? What's happened, then?

MOLLY. It's Winnie, she's passed out.

KEVIN. Well what was all that now?

GASTON. The heat. Always affecting someone. Terrible.

> (*Meanwhile . . .*)

PETER (*to* MONIQUE). Did you—er—you still going to do it. I mean I . . .

MONIQUE. Don't worry Peter, I shall see to it now. It's not the first time is it?

PETER. You don't think we should go through with it? I don't mind being responsible. After all it is my baby.

MONIQUE. Enough, I'm not going to talk about it any more.

PETER. You told Monty about us then?

MONIQUE. You really must stop rowing with Marango, darling.

PETER. Did you speak to Monty as we said?

MONIQUE. They won't stand it all the time, you know. I'm always telling you about this, Peter.

PETER. Listen Monique, I love you. Please listen to me that I love you. You said you love me but you don't say to your husband this thing.

HETTIE (*to* FRANK). Two chicken.

MONIQUE. Now not this again.

PETER. You are not going to leave him are you? You don't really intend to?

MONIQUE. Oh Peter, please.

PETER. What do you want I should do then?

MONIQUE. Did the Chef say much?

PETER. We could leave any day. We could go for a long holiday first. Ski-ing in Switzerland perhaps.

MONIQUE. I am going to the hairdresser tomorrow as well.

PETER. Monique, we row this morning, we row in the afternoon too, this evening we are almost in love again . . . Answer me.

MONIQUE. Did I tell you Monty's going to buy me a house?

PETER (*screaming*). Monique!

> (MONIQUE *looks round in embarrassment and, muttering* 'You fool,' *stalks off.* VIOLET *approaches* PETER.)

VIOLET (*subdued—to* PETER). You serving yet, Peter? I want three turbot. Special for Marango.

PETER. It's half past six yet?

VIOLET. It's nearly . . .

PETER. Half past six is service.

VIOLET. But it's special . . .

PETER. Half past six!

DAPHNE (*to* HANS). Two sausages.

> (*Service is just beginning. Evening service is not so hectic and takes a longer time to start up. Waitresses appear, most people are at their stations.*)

BETTY (*to* KEVIN). Two plaice.

KEVIN. Me, I'd have a Jaguar. It's got a luxury I could live with.

GASTON. Have you seen the new French Citroën? Just like a mechanical frog it looks.

HANS. And the Volkswagen? It's not a good car?

KEVIN. Now there's a good little car for little money.

HANS. No country makes like the Volkswagen.

KEVIN. You've gotta hand it to the Germans.

> (*More waitresses are coming in, but the service is easy and orders ring out in comfort.* CYNTHIA, *however, breaks her journey round the kitchen, and, with a glass of wine, goes up to the* CHEF *to gossip.* MAX *and* NICHOLAS *stand by listening.*)

CYNTHIA. Heard what happened to Winnie? She's been rushed to hospital.

MAX. What did she do wrong then?

CYNTHIA. She was pregnant.

MAX. She didn't look it.

CYNTHIA. I know. She didn't give herself a chance.

CHEF. Misfired?

CYNTHIA. I'll say, and it weren't no accident neither.

MAX (*shaking his head*). Silly woman, silly woman.

CHEF. She's got seven children already, though.

CYNTHIA. That's right. Marango's hopping mad. It started happening on the spot, in there, in the dining-room. May and Sophie had to take her away.

MAX. What did she do, then?

CYNTHIA. She took pills, that's what. And I'll tell you something else, there are four other girls here took the same pills. There! Four of them!

BETTY (*to* HANS). Two veal cutlets.

CYNTHIA. And you know who one of the four is ? (*She inclines her head in Peter's direction.*)

MAX. Monique ?

CYNTHIA (*nodding her head triumphantly*). Now don't you tell anyone I told you, mind. But you ask Hettie, ask her, she bought the stuff. (*Continues on the round to* KEVIN.) Two plaice, please.

GWEN (*to* HANS). Two hamburgers.

MAX. Knew this would happen.

HETTIE. Two halibut. (*This is said to* PETER, *who sits on stool centre, back to audience.*)

MAX. Knew it. Can't be done, though. What makes them think that by taking a tablet through the mouth it will affect the womb.

HETTIE. Oh come on Peter, two halibut.

    (PETER *slowly rises to serve her.*)

MAX. There's only one way, the way it went in . . . What happens with a tablet ? Nothing . . . Nothing can.

    (PETER *serves only one halibut.*)

HETTIE (*to* PETER). I said two.

MAX. The stomach is irritated, that's all, squeezed see ? Forces the womb. Presses it.

NICHOLAS. Now what do you know about this ? A doctor now!

MAX. Oh I know about this all right. Only one drug is effective through the mouth. (*secretively*) And you know what that is ? Ergot ? Heard of it ? Only thing to do it. And that's rare. Oh yes, I studied this in the forces when I had nothing else to do. Very interesting, this psychology. Complicated. I knew Winnie was in pod as soon as she came here.

    (*All the time, the pastrycooks have been clearing away their* station and are now ready to go. *They are saying goodbye to everyone.* MAX *shouts to them as they go.*)

MAX. Some people have it easy!

(*The pastrycooks begin to leave, and, as they do so, an argument flares up suddenly at* PETER'S *station.*)

MOLLY (*to* HANS). Two sausages.

GWEN (*to* PETER). One turbot.

DAPHNE (*to* PETER). Three cod.

PETER. It's not ready yet.

DAPHNE. Oh come on Peter, three cod.

PETER. It's not ready yet, come back five minutes' time.

(*All the other chefs sing* 'Hi lee, hi lo, hi la' *at him.*)

MOLLY (*to* HANS). Four veal cutlets.

GWEN (*to* PETER). Six turbot.

JACKIE (*to* PETER). Two halibut.

VIOLET (*to* PETER). Two turbot. (*As there is a queue she tries to help herself.*)

PETER (*to* VIOLET). You wait for me yes? *I* serve you. You ask *me*.

VIOLET. But you were busy.

PETER. I don't care. This is my place and there (*points to the side of bar*), there is for you.

VIOLET. Now you wait a bloody minute will you? Who the hell do you think you are, you?

PETER. You don't worry who I am. I'm the cook yes? And you're the waitress, and in the kitchen I do what I like yes? And in the dining-room you do what you like.

VIOLET (*taking another plate from off the oven*). I won't take orders from you, you know, I . . .

PETER (*shouting and smashing the plate from her hand for a second time*). Leave it! Leave it there! I'll serve you. Me! Me! Is *my* kingdom here. This is the side where *I* live. This.

VIOLET (*very quietly*). You Boche you. You bloody German bastard!

(*She downs plates on the bar and walks off.* PETER *follows her. There is a general uproar and protest from the other waitresses who are waiting to be served.*)

PETER. What you call me? What was it? Say it again. (*He screams at her.*) SAY IT AGAIN! (*She halts, petrified.*)

(*The scream calls the attention of most people to him. They all stare at him as at a frightened animal. Suddenly he wheels round and in a frenzy searches for something violent to do. He rushes up to* VIOLET. *Seems about to attack her, but she is not the enemy. He knocks plates off one of the counters. Other chefs rush to hold him. He breaks away and reaches for a large chopper. Everyone backs away. Then with a cry of* 'auf geht's,' *he dashes to a part under a serving-counter and smashes something underneath. There is a slow hiss and all the fires of the ovens die down. There is a second of complete silence before anybody realizes what has happened, and then* FRANK *and two others are upon him, trying to hold him down. The* CHEF, *at last moved to do something, rushes to the scene, but* PETER *breaks away again and flees to the dining-room.* FRANK *and others follow. All this has happened too quickly for anyone to do a great deal about it, but in the scuffle the following cries were heard—*)

MICHAEL. He's broken the gas lead! Someone turn off the main!

(MANGOLIS *exits to do so.*)

FRANK. Hold him, grab hold of him!

KEVIN. Jesus Christ he'll murder her.

HANS. Sei nicht dumm! Beherrsch dich! Lass sie laufen!

(*When* PETER *has rushed into the dining-room, there is another silence as everybody waits to hear what will happen next. Some are not even sure what has already happened. Suddenly there is a tremendous crash of crockery and glass to the ground. There are screams, some waitresses come back into kitchen from dining-room.*)

KEVIN. Holy mother o' Mary, he's gone berserk.

GASTON. The lunatic! He's swept all the plates off the table in there.

MICHAEL. He's ripped his hands.

KEVIN. I knew something like this would happen, now I just knew it.

(*The crowd by the entrance to the dining-room makes way as* ALFREDO *and* HANS *bring* PETER *back.* PETER'S *hands are covered in blood. Some smears have reached his face. He looks terribly exhausted. They bring him down stage.* MICHAEL *hurriedly finds a stool.*)

CHEF (*to* MICHAEL). Phone an ambulance.

WAITRESS. Monique is doing that now.

(MONIQUE *pushes through the crowd. She is sobbing but she carries the medical box and a table-cloth.* ALFREDO *snatches the cloth from her and rips it up. She tries to dab some liquid on* PETER'S *hands, he jumps and pushes her away. This is too much for her; she leaves it all and rushes away.* ALFREDO, *however, simply takes* PETER'S *hands and ties them up.*)

PETER. It hurts, Christ it hurts.

ALFREDO. Shut up!

CHEF (*bending close to* PETER). Fool! (*He straightens up, and, finding nothing else to say for the moment, bends down to repeat again.*) Fool! (*Pause.*) So? What? The whole kitchen is stopped. Fool!

PETER (*to* ALFREDO). Now he cares.

CHEF (*incredulous and furious*). What do you mean, 'Now he cares'?

ALFREDO (*gently moving* CHEF *out of the way so that he might tie up* PETER'S *hands*). Leave him Chef, leave him now.

CHEF (*reaching* PETER *another way*). What do you mean, 'Now he cares'? *You* have to make me care? Forty years and suddenly you have to make me care? You? You? Who are you, tell me? In all this big world who are you for Christ's sake?

(*At this point the crowd breaks away to let* MARANGO *in. He surveys the damage.*)

MARANGO (*with terrible calm*). You have stopped my whole world. (*Pause.*) Did you get permission from God? Did you? There—is—no—one—else! You know that? NO ONE!

FRANK. All right, take it easy Marango. The boy is going, he's going. He's ill, don't upset yourself.

MARANGO (*turning to* FRANK *and making a gentle appeal*). Why does everybody sabotage me, Frank? I give work, I pay well, yes? They eat what they want, don't they? I don't know what more to give a man. He works, he eats, I give him money. This is life, isn't it? I haven't made a mistake, have I? I live in the right world, don't I? (*to* PETER) And you've stopped this world. A shnip! A boy! You've stopped it. Well why? Maybe you can tell me something I don't know—just tell me. (*No answer.*) I want to learn something. (*to the kitchen*) Is there something I don't know? (PETER *rises and in pain moves off. When he reaches a point back centre stage* MARANGO *cries at him.*) BLOODY FOOL! (*Rushes round to him.*) What more do you want? What is there more, tell me? (*He shakes* PETER, *but gets no reply.* PETER *again tries to leave. Again* MARANGO *cries out.*) What is there more? (PETER *stops, turns in pain and sadness, shakes his head as if to say—'if you don't know, I cannot explain'. And so he moves right off stage.* MARANGO *is left facing his staff, who stand around, almost accusingly, looking at him. And he asks again—*) What is there more? What is there more? What is there more?

Introduction to

SOLDIER, SOLDIER—*John Arden*

THE PLAYWRIGHT AND HIS WORK

John Arden is unusual among present writers in that he does
not write autobiographically. He uses a wide range of material
as subjects for his plays. They remain plays of ideas of general
social or moral issues, more than plays about strongly developed
characters. There are times however when he draws upon his
background for the detail of his plays while remaining objective
about it throughout. Although John Arden now lives away
from the North, he still retains strong traces of his northern
upbringing and a clear sense of community. He was born in
1930 in Barnsley and went to a local elementary school. Then
when the war came he went to Sedburgh School in the York-
shire Dales and it was here that he made his decision to train
as an architect.

From here he studied at Cambridge University and then
spent two years at the College of Art in Edinburgh. Then for a
while he worked in an architect's office in London. At this time
his writing was developing. He had written various plays in
both verse and prose, including a kind of academic exercise in
the style of *Samson Agonistes* about the death of Hitler. He had
also had a period comedy, *All Fall Down*, about the building of
a railway, performed by his fellow students at Edinburgh. But
it wasn't until he submitted a play *Life of Man* to a BBC
North Region competition that he first attracted notice. George
Devine at the Royal Court Theatre invited him to write for the
English Stage Company. The first play he offered them was
rejected but they gave *The Waters of Babylon* a performance as
one of their productions on a low budget, 'without decor'. This

did not receive much acclaim. In fact Arden can never claim to have had 'rave' notices. Most of his work the critics have found rather boring for he has a strong distrust of attitudes. Instead of taking sides or making the characters act as his mouthpiece, he prefers to examine people, situations and ideas, not to point out which are right and which are wrong. He therefore does not draw heroes and villains in the accepted sense, and frequently leaves his audience facing the problem and unable to tell where his own sympathy lies.

While on his honeymoon John Arden wrote his next play which was *Soldier, Soldier*. He was interested in folk music and the ballad tradition and in this play he built the whole drama upon the idea behind the song. He felt he wanted to try his hand at writing for television. At that time he did not know much about the medium but had spent some time at the television studios watching a play being rehearsed. It was, he says, a rather off-putting experience, as during transmission one of the cameras broke down and near-panic broke loose. He came away with a clear awareness of the hazards of the medium but not much help about its potential.

After this he wrote a play called *Live Like Pigs* in which a group of gipsy folk who are both unruly and disreputable move into a semi-detached housing estate and disturb the complacency of the settled and respectable Jacksons.

Then in 1959 came *Sergeant Musgrave's Dance*, still his most widely acclaimed play and that most closely associated with his name. The setting is a northern town in the 1880s to which Sergeant Musgrave comes apparently recruiting but really to teach the townsfolk a lesson about war.

In a way each of Arden's plays is an experiment both with playwriting methods and with ideas. While holding the playwriting fellowship at Bristol University he wrote a play using half masks, *Happy Haven*—a grotesque comedy of old age and rejuvenation. He has explored *The Business of Good Government* not just in this, his version of the Christmas Story but also in some of his other plays—notably *The Workhouse Donkey* produced at Chichester in 1963.

He has tried his hand at all kinds of approaches to dramatic writing but nearly always remains close to the ballad tradition. He is a conscious craftsman and an artist. Each time he writes he explores with freshness and originality. At one and the same time he reaches out to traditions of the past (particularly Shakespeare and the Elizabethans) and forges into the present and the future attempting to create a popular theatre about the important concerns of today.

It may be useful to read the play at this point before continuing with the introduction.

THEME AND CHARACTERS

Something of the atmosphere of the play is set by the ballad on which it is based. The soldier of the song is getting all he can from the girl; she is hoping for his hand in marriage until he finally reveals the truth:

> 'Oh, no, sweet maid, I cannot marry you
> for I have a wife of my own!'

But Arden does more, much more than give us a lively comedy about the characters of the original song. He presents us with a situation which unfolds and challenges attitudes. The Soldier of the play is a loud, uncontrollable 'con' man who strides, almost dances, into the rather settled community of a northern industrial town. We are presented on the one hand with the representative of disorder and anarchy—the Soldier who cons and deceives: on the other we have the forces of order in terms of established complacency—the Scuffhams living their conventionally narrow existence. It is not a question simply of right and wrong, it is a question also of incompatibility. The Soldier—notice he is never given a name—arrives late at this northern town and swaggers into the local pub. He cannot, will not, be ignored and before very long his vitality and apparent self-confidence, his bravado and ebullience has won its way into the hearts of the occupants of the dreary working-class tavern. Even when we see the Soldier lie and inveigle his way into the Scuffham's household we still seem to find him attractive. It is obvious to us that he is trading on the ignorance of the folk, with his story that he knows their son and can help restore him to his newly married wife again. It is not long before he is given lordly treatment, breakfast in bed, and is eventually able to seduce Mary and extract a fair amount of the family's life savings.

Neither the Parkers nor the Scuffhams are very fully drawn but we learn sufficient of them to appreciate them in their environment. They hold views against war in an abstract sort of way. Parker says: 'Indeed, I'd go so far as to say as my principles don't hold with the Army' (p. 168), and Scuffham in bitterness speaks of his son, 'When he went for a Regular soldier, he threw up everything I tried to learn him' (p. 172).

Both families try to work on the soul of Mary. 'We've tried to get her to change and to go for *proper* religion' (p. 173), says Mrs. Scuffham. But their views are as set as their ways and they really have no insight or understanding of others. They live at the gossip level passing on items of news of this or that person but never really going beyond the surface in attempting to appreciate motives or feelings. 'You take Ethel Hopkins for an instance. Her boy, he was in the Air Force in the war, and he went and he got married in Southampton ... well, I *mean ...*' (p. 190).

The Soldier uses them in their ignorance to get all he can from them, but they, in spite of their chapel and religion and principles, are just as keen to use the Soldier if they think it will help their advancement: 'Now, you listen to me, Charlie. Everything's lovely, it's all arranged.' (p. 201). Parker explains that he has been to the Mayor at the Trades Union Offices and this important man, 'He's more than just Mayor; he's like Napoleon in this wappentake—Council, committees, unions and all—and he says to me, "Joe," he says, "Joe, that soldier's worth a mine of black diamonds, in the right place. I want our M.P. to meet him," he says.' (p. 201). And so Parker is delighted at his catch and truly believes that his political future is made—'Councillor Parker soon. Then Alderman. *Then* what?' (p. 201).

In her bedroom Mary broods apart over her toy soldier and shows more apparent readiness to respond on a level beyond the mundane. She seems to have become trapped by circumstances and the community in which she now lives but she has dreams which will take her away. She partly sees through the Soldier and she also sees her own opportunity: 'You took the money because you told them lies, but I tell you no lies: I'm coming with you, soldier, and I'm living with you and that money's my only fortune and we're travelling today.' (p. 208). But she does not know him well enough and true to the ballad he leaves her, 'Ye can keep the whistle, keep it: dance yourself a jig, whiles. Hech, ye're a bonny lassie: but I telled ye that, last evening . . . Good-bye to ye so.' (p. 211). In a way that is his good-bye to all the community. He has given them some music and made them pay for it—they have had some life and entertainment but none of them seem very much wiser for it.

STYLE AND PRODUCTION

The awareness of the need for social change is presented at a double distance. First of all, we step back and look at the questions raised and try to define the issues further through the comedy: we remain outside and unemotionally involved when we laugh. Secondly, the use of a great deal of very clear verse form and song rhymes helps us to remove the situation further from immediate reality. Arden feels that writing which is only half verse presents difficulty to an audience but argues that they are not worried if they are clear about the form being used. Here he employs verse with a strong beat and occasionally rhyme to heighten certain parts of the play. As in some

Shakespearean plays, Arden uses prose for the most every-day comedy and writes in verse when he wants to suggest a different kind of world. So the form of the play helps to emphasize the contrasts both of character and attitude. Arden has a keen sense of rhythm and in reading and acting out the play, the more sensitively these are appreciated, the better will be the impact. The music is an integral part and should not thumb its way into the action.

As with the Henry Livings' television play, so here the script could be acted following the convention strictly as it is written, imagining the camera if one is not available. But this play too, is easily seen in terms of live theatre with only elementary modifications. Hardly any setting is required and only the simplest of properties. If it is presented in perform-ance, lighting can help define the areas, and for classroom work, different parts of the room can be mapped out as: the tavern, the street, the Scuffham's living room, Mary's bedroom. This will enable the action to flow easily and the dialogue will make clear the time at which the events take place.

Arden says in his introduction to the first printed version of the play that the 'success it had was due to its comic or satiric qualities, to its use of music, to the talent of the cast and to the raucous vitality of Stuart Burge's production'. The acting talent called for is a clear sense of the roles. These can be fairly 'stock' but not so stereotyped as to lose the link with reality. Some carefully chosen items of costume will help the establish-ment of truth. The inhabitants of the community would do well to work out some improvisations together about the kind of lives they lead. Scenes linked with chapel, the neighbours, the trade union meetings and the Council committees should be worked out. This kind of work will prove invaluable in creating an ensemble style of playing and help to suggest the unity of attitude seen in the town. The Soldier and Mary could carry out improvisations apart from the others so that when the whole cast eventually comes together we would more easily appreciate the outsiders. The Soldier needs to sense his Aldershot training and discipline so that he can more readily enjoy the freedom of the night away from barracks and know why anarchy is so enjoyable. Mary could act out scenes of her parting with her new husband and her isolation from friends and home.

Then in the rehearsals for the play itself the quality of 'raucous vitality' needs to be worked for. This will come not only from the Soldier but also from the townsfolk who need to act out their parts with boldness and a sense of pace. Even though they lead dull lives, they, as people, are presented as comic and therefore interesting to those watching. Even the most colloquial sections are written with a sense of life which is conveyed through the rhythm.

Soldier, Soldier

JOHN ARDEN

Soldier, Soldier was first presented by BBC Television on 16 February 1960.

Street.
Music: 'Soldier, Soldier' played very vigorous on drums and fifes.
A pair of feet in well-bulled army boots and tartan trews striding along a stone-sett street.
Sound of railway trains, etc.
A pub at the corner, to which the owner of the feet (the SOLDIER*) is rapidly making his way, his back to the camera.*
He goes with a fine flash swagger, twirling his little cane. It is dusk.

Inside the pub.
Close-up of an engraved-glass panel at the top of a door reading 'Railway Arms': 'Public Bar'. The door swings open and crashes shut.
The screen is filled with the back view of the SOLDIER *as he strides across the floor to the bar counter.*
The LANDLORD *is busy polishing his counter and glasses.*
The SOLDIER *stops, facing the* LANDLORD, *who is too occupied to serve him for the moment.*
The music stops, and we hear the various strands of conversation from the as yet invisible customers.

FIRST VOICE. Aye now, but you look at it this road: a centre-half's a centre-half, I mean choose what . . .
SECOND VOICE. You can't call him a full-back . . .
THIRD VOICE. I tell you he was a sick man at the time. Bound to distort his judgement.
FOURTH VOICE. Never lifted his head, never lifted his head again . . . Take it which way you like.
SOLDIER (*suddenly lifts his chin and bellows*). Git on parade!
(*All the talking stops.*)
One-two-three, two-two three, Three!

(He beats both fists on the bar, and shouts all in a gabble):

> Who comes here?
> A Fusilier,
> What does he want?
> He wants his beer.
> Where's his money?
> Here's his money.

(He tosses a pocketful of miscellaneous money on to the bar, and exhorts the LANDLORD.*)*
Smarten it up, mucker, there's a soldier wants his drink.

We now see the rest of the room and its occupants. It is a dreary little working-class tavern, with only a few customers.
These are all men, mostly elderly and nondescript, sitting or standing in small gloomy groups.
One man, JOE PARKER, *is at a table alone. He is about fifty, short, bald and seedy, with an inquisitive twitching nose and a Hitler moustache. His suit has a buttoned-up air of down-at-heel respectability, and he wears a collar and tie. His hat is an old black Homburg.*

LANDLORD *(sour)*. There's a soldier's *had* his drink, if you ask me . . . All right, all right, chum, what'll it be?
SOLDIER. Stingo.
LANDLORD. Stingo.
SOLDIER. Stingo.
LANDLORD. Pint?
SOLDIER. Pint.
LANDLORD. Pint you are then . . . Steady, mucker, easy steady with it now.

The SOLDIER *is lifting the glass high up in front of him with both hands.*
The LANDLORD *watches this operation apprehensively. The* SOLDIER *slowly carries it to its zenith, then tilts it suddenly and deftly pours the contents into his mouth.*

SOLDIER.

Easy steady up she goes . . .

Up and over

The walls of Dover:

Here we go down into Folkestone town.

(*The glass is drained in one operation. He sets it down and takes a great breath. There is some mild applause. The* SOLDIER *turns round, leans back against the bar, and surveys the room. For the first time we see his face. He is a big tall man of thirty-five, with black hair and fierce hatchet features. He is dressed very smartly in tartan trews, blue walking-out tunic and a blue Balmoral bonnet. His accent is hard lowland Scots.*)

This is no flaming Folkestone, this town.

Where stands the man'll

Tell me the name of *this* town ?

LANDLORD. Not know the name of it, mucker ?

SOLDIER.

Not know the name of it.

How should I know the name ?

All that I did was get out of a train.

'What station's this one ?' I asked him,

I asked him on the platform . . .

Now where I want to get to . . .

I want to get to Aldershot.

LANDLORD. We're over two hundred miles from Aldershot.

SOLDIER.

But I only got off for a cup of tea;

I only got off for a sandwich.

Two minutes only to get a cup of . . .

I've gone and missed the train.

How can I get to Aldershot tonight ?

LANDLORD. Oh, you'll not be able to now, while tomorrow morning. You'll be able to stop here, mate. You ought to have looked sharp, you ought. They never wait long for you at this station, y'know. It's not even always what they call a scheduled stop.

SOLDIER.

>Stay here? Stay where?
>Did I not say a sandwich!
>Never a man alive tonight
>To sell me one sandwich.
>What sort of toss-eyed town . . .

(*He suddenly beats his fists again on the bar.*)
Stingo!

The LANDLORD *refills his glass, and he drinks it moodily, slumped over the bar.*
The general conversation now resumes.

FIRST VOICE. How many seasons has he played, you tell me that?

SECOND VOICE. That's nowt but evading the point; he's done and he's done. Politics is politics.

THIRD VOICE. And that's all there is to it.

FIRST VOICE. How many seasons?

FOURTH VOICE. Well, you take Churchill now, I mean take him and look at him . . .

PARKER *has not taken his eyes off the* SOLDIER.

PARKER. There's a train about ten o'clock in t'morning, Serjeant: take you via London.

SOLDIER (*who is a private*).

>Serjeant he calls me. Serjeant.
>So hear him he gives praise
>To the glory where it's due.
>The Lord preserve ye for that word, man,
>Prosperity be yours
>And uncounted Posterity.

(*He swings round at the* LANDLORD.)

Do *you* hold any sandwich?

One sandwich in this house?

LANDLORD (*shaking his head*). Potato crisps. Pickled gherkin. Popcorn.

SOLDIER (*disgusted*).

>Nor never one sandwich

>Ham, egg, nor cheese,

>For a solitary travelling man.

PARKER (*suddenly*). Caledonian Fusiliers.

SOLDIER (*sharply*). What?

PARKER. Aye? Am I right? I'll tell you: I thought I knew the badge.

SOLDIER (*fiercely contemptuous*).

>Ye thought ye knew the badge.

>Ye thought ye knew the . . .

>Hey, mucker, hey, will I tell ye about this badge!

(*He grips* PARKER *by the lapel, and, taking off his bonnet, thrusts the badge into his eyes.*)

>Caledonian Fusiliers.

A DRINKER (*to another*). Warn't that the regiment that Charlie Scuffham's lad joined up in?

SECOND DRINKER. Nay, I don't know . . .

FIRST DRINKER. I reckon it was. Eh, what a cockeyed business that affair, warn't it . . .

SOLDIER.

>Observe there's words set down, it's a motto,

>Can ye read it, hey, can ye read?

PARKER (*flurried*). Wait, steady on, Serjeant . . .

SOLDIER (*relentless*). There's important words are here set down . . .

PARKER (*nervously appeasing*).

>Aye, I know: I can see them.

>Wrote – like – in Scotch, isn't it, Serjeant?

>Very interesting.

>Fa fa, what is it, fo fa . . .

SOLDIER (*grandly*).

> 'Foul may fa' oor foes thegither.'
> Or in plain Saxon, mucker,
> 'Here's two fists of clouds of thunder:
> Stand out of their road
> Because there's lightnings dance between them!'

(*He has replaced his bonnet on his head, and now thrusts his clenched fists under* PARKER'S *nose.*)

> Two fists of a Fusilier:
> Two fists of the only regiment
> Has never ever even once been beat.
> Except that time by the Frenchman;
> But then there was a war.

LANDLORD. What about the other times?

SOLDIER (*whirling round*). What other times?

LANDLORD.

> When there warn't no war.
> When there was nowt but peaceful shepherds
> To never ever beat you.

A voice down the room among laughter.

A VOICE. Tell us about them shepherds, mate, eh.

SOLDIER.

> Aye, man, I'll tell ye.
> But first I will finish the drink:
> Get good beer beneath your middle
> Ye'll fight like a horse
> And sing like a fiddle.

While the SOLDIER *finishes his drink, one* DRINKER *leans against the bar at the far end of it and watches him humorously.*

DRINKER (*to no one in particular*).

> All them peaceable shepherds, he says.
> Eh, the Army, *I* don't know . . .

(*The* DRINKER *laughs and beckons the* LANDLORD.)

(*Confidentially*). What's up with Nosey Parker tonight? It's not as a general rule he wants to talk to soldiers.

LANDLORD (*also confidentially*). Unless about his principles. We've not heard overmuch about them principles tonight, have we?

DRINKER. I wonder why not.

LANDLORD (*significantly*). Caledonian Fusiliers.

DRINKER. Eh?

LANDLORD. It's not over often you see Scotchmen in this town, and specially Fusiliers.

DRINKER. What are you talking about?

LANDLORD. Old Charlie Scuffham, the window-cleaner. What was the name of that young lad of his?

DRINKER. Oh, you mean Tommy Scuffham?

LANDLORD. Aye, Tommy. *You* know.

DRINKER (*apparently enlightened*). Oh. Oh, aye.

LANDLORD (*suddenly looking up, alarmed*). Watch out, mate, watch out . . .

The SOLDIER *comes sweeping down along the front of the bar, pushing the* DRINKER *roughly out of his way.*

SOLDIER. Ho-ho –

LANDLORD. Now wait a minute, wait a minute . . .

SOLDIER (*waving a bottle in a wild attitude*).

> Ho-ho, boys, I'll tell yous.
> The noble battle-honours, my boys,
> Of the Caledonian Fusiliers.
> Serve every man a drink:
> There's all of my silver
> There on the timber!

(*The* LANDLORD *rather dubious. But as the company come forward with their empty glasses, murmuring gratefully, he begins to serve them all.*

The SOLDIER *has assumed a rhetorical attitude for his narra-*
tion, though once or twice during it he breaks off and moves
about the room, clapping people on the back and generally
seizing their attention.)

Nineteen thirty-nine:
I join with the regiment.
Ye'll remember, next year,
Beaches of Dunkirk;
We're against a Scots Guards company,
All fists and feet, boy . . .
Puts their CSM to hospital
And a Provost-Corporal no teeth left.
Every man a drink!
Nineteen forty-one, where were we then?
Catterick, och aye, the old Tank Corps
Twelve with broken ribs
And three for psychiatric treatment.
Six of our own boys
Northallerton Glasshouse.
Christmas forty-two,
Recapture of Tobruk,
The Australian fighting Army:
Never looked up after that day:
Chased 'em fifty miles.
Forty-three, Forty-four
Africa and Italy.
Matched against the Yanks
The most of that time.
They'd never a chance
With those rubber-soled boots, man.
We knew the game to give 'em.
And the Polack soldiers too.
We showed 'em where.
Polacks fought beside us once:
Against the Free French Navy:

    Drowned them in dozens.

    They used knives, the Polacks.

    Then after the war . . .

PARKER (*thrusting forward*). After the war.

SOLDIER (*savagely*). I'm talking, mucker.

PARKER.

    Aye, but after the war.

    Were you ever in Germany?

SOLDIER.

    Himmelherrgottkreuzmillionendonnerwetter!

    Were *we* ever in Germany!

    Who were the boys

    Set Düsseldorf Naafi club on fire?

    Who stole the Burgomaster's daughter

    Out of Bacharach-on-Rhine?

    There was a song made over that:

    I'm going to sing it to yous.

    Shut your mouths, every man.

(*He jumps up on to a table and begins to sing in a strong but not untuneable voice. Air: 'The Reformed Rake'.*)

    'My father he told me

    Never go with the soldiers,

    Never go with the soldiers,

    O my daughter dear.

    I swore to obey him,

    Little thought how this morning

    I'd wake in the arms

    Of my fine Fusilier.'

(*The* LANDLORD *is looking at his watch. Acknowledging applause*):

    There was more verses, aye,

    But they've gone from my mind.

LANDLORD. All right, it's Time, everybody, Time! Who can take a hint, eh? *Time* is what I said –

SOLDIER.

> So instead I'll play the tune to yous
> On my old tin whistle.

He produces a penny whistle from his pocket.

LANDLORD (*his hand on the light switches*). Half past ten. *I've* got the law to keep, soldier, whatever you may be thinking of doing.

(*The* SOLDIER *makes a rude noise at the* LANDLORD. *He plays the tune on his whistle, and performs a little step-dance on the table.*)

All right then. All right.

The LANDLORD *switches the lights out, leaving the room illuminated by the bar light only.*

SOLDIER (*violently*).

> All right then yourself then, mucker.
> Up the Fusiliers.

He jumps down from the table, and sweeps a row of glasses to the floor with his arm.
Close-up of a bottle smashing into a mirror.
Shouting, running feet, police whistles. Silence.

The corner of a street.
The street is dark and empty, save for the SOLDIER, *who leans against a lamp-post playing 'The Reformed Rake' on his whistle, and speaking to the moon between each line of the music.*

SOLDIER.

> I've missed my train to Aldershot . . . (*Music*)
> No money for a bed . . . (*Music*)
> I hit a yelping polisman . . . (*Music*)
> With a bottle on the head.

Am I no a dandy travelling soldier?
I cannot even tell ye the name of this town.

PARKER (*from off-screen*).

Well it's not Folkestone nor Dover.
And it's not Inverness, Serjeant,
I can tell you that's true.

PARKER *comes forward out of the shadows. The* SOLDIER
looks at him sardonically.

SOLDIER. And *you're* not my Uncle Alexander and I'm not a Minister of the Free Kirk and who the hell are ye anyway?

PARKER. My name's Parker, Serjeant.

SOLDIER. Indeed. Nosey Parker, I dare well say.

PARKER. There's no call for discourtesy, you know. I did you a favour getting you out of that public.

SOLDIER. Awa' with your favours.

PARKER. Now then, now then . . .

SOLDIER. I am seeking my own society the night. I need no man's favourings.

PARKER. You've missed your train to Aldershot; there's not another while morning. What'll they do to you when you get there a day late?

SOLDIER (*matter-of-fact*). The usual, they'll do. 'Cap and belt off, witness – accused – escort 'tenshun, left turn, right turn, quick-march leftright leftright leftright, left wheel right wheel, mark time leftright leftright leftright . . . Halt!' 'Twenty-four hours absent without leave have you anything to say?' 'Permission to speak, sir? Nothing to say, sir.' 'How many more times are you going to be brought up before me on this sort of charge, most unsatisfactory, seven days detention three days loss of pay Royal Warrant, march him out, Sarnt-major.' 'Seven days detention three days Royal Warrant leftright leftright leftright . . . Halt!' God send us all good ending.

PARKER (*extremely impressed*). It's wicked, it's right wicked any lad should suffer that.

SOLDIER. A very honest opinion, mucker. Vastly does ye credit.

The SOLDIER *starts to play on his whistle again, clearly wishing to be rid of the other.*

PARKER *dithers about for a moment, then decides to reopen the conversation.*

PARKER. You, er – got anywhere to stay tonight?

SOLDIER. Not that I know.

PARKER. There's no question of your not having enough to pay for a bed, though, is there?

SOLDIER. Is there? Isn't there? What makes ye imagine that?

PARKER (*insinuating*). Well now, Serjeant, I saw all that brass you was broadcasting out on bar counter. I'm not blind.

SOLDIER (*sharply*). No? But ye're no so perspicacious, I dare venture, as to look clear into the pooches of a man's breeks, and reckon precisely just what silver remains there, hey?

(*He puts his hand in his trews pocket and pulls out a few coins, which he holds out for* PARKER'S *inspection.*)

Two shillings and fivepence ha'penny, and what the devil is it to you?

PARKER (*suddenly*). Do you know Tommy Scuffham?

SOLDIER (*carelessly*). I do not.

PARKER. Not in Germany?

SOLDIER. Never heard of him.

PARKER (*rather dashed*). Eh, dear . . .

SOLDIER. What d'ye mean. 'Eh, dear'?

PARKER. Now look, Serjeant, I'm not a military man, you know . . .

SOLDIER. I'll believe that.

PARKER. Indeed, I'd go so far as to say as my principles don't hold with the Army . . . er, that's not personal you know, no offence, no offence. We all have our views, don't we, entitled to our own views, but you, er – ah the fact is –

(*The* SOLDIER *walks away from him, but* PARKER *trots round in front and prevents his escape.*)

You see, Charlie Scuffham he cleans the windows, he's a very old friend of mine. Aye, and his wife, too, our Ida, that is, Ida Scuffham, you know . . .

SOLDIER (*sings: tune as before*).

'My father he told me
If you go with the soldiers
They'll lead you a journey
Of sin and of shame . . .'

PARKER. And it's over two years now since they heard a single word of him – well, I mean they're fair worried about it, bound to be, it's only nature, isn't it?

SOLDIER (*sings*).

'And if I go back to
The house where they reared me,
How can I face up
To such merited blame?'

PARKER (*still pursuing*). You see I thought – like – this Tommy Scuffham, if you'd ever heard of him, if you'd heard a word of him and you told them about it, his mum and dad and Mary, you know – I mean you're in same regiment, after all, I thought you might have known . . .

SOLDIER (*vaguely*). Regiment, whose regiment? . . .

(*The* SOLDIER *ponders a moment, looking at* PARKER *as though he has not heard what he has been saying until this minute. He leans against a doorway, looking up to the sky, and appears to reminisce.*)

Johnny Scruff – Och aye, Johnny Scuffham. God, he was the boy.

PARKER (*gently*). Tommy Scuffham.

SOLDIER (*carelessly*). Och aye, Tommy. We always called him Johnny. God, he was the boy.

PARKER. Aye, but what's happened to him, that's what we
. . .

SOLDIER (*mysteriously*). Happened to him? Aha – *there's* a question, mucker.

PARKER. Aye, but . . .

SOLDIER. *There* is a question . . . Mary?

PARKER. That's right. She's his wife.

SOLDIER. Will *I* put a question to *you* then? Have *you* got a wife?

PARKER (*taken aback*). Me?

SOLDIER. You.

PARKER. I've got a wife.

SOLDIER (*clapping him on the shoulder*). Then ye're a marvellous man, mucker. Lead me to her.

PARKER (*even more taken aback*). My wife?

SOLDIER (*cheerfully*). Och no. Tommy's wife, Johnny's Mary, mum, dad, and the kailyard cock. That's a very interesting question ye put: what's happened to Johnny. Tommy?

PARKER. Tommy.

SOLDIER. Ha!

The SOLDIER *plays 'Soldier, Soldier' on his whistle, and the two of them march off down the deserted street.*

MARY'S *bedroom, in the* SCUFFHAMS' *house.*
Close-up of a toy soldier on a chair, and a pair of hands playing with it.
They are MARY'S *hands, and we now see her face. During this scene her whole person and the room are gradually revealed. She is a girl in her early twenties, tidily yet dowdily dressed. Her general appearance is rather slow and cow-like – an impression belied by the intensity of her eyes. She is not a big girl, but her movements are gauche and self-conscious.*
She is lying stretched out on her stomach on an ugly brass bedstead. The other furniture in the little room consists of a wash-stand with jug and basin and a chest of drawers. The room is untidy

*and littered with clothes, etc., but the chest of drawers has nothing
on top of it save a cheap plaster statue of the madonna and child
and a little bowl of flowers in front. It is after dark and the naked
electric bulb in the ceiling is lit.*

MARY (*sings quietly. Air: 'Soldier, Soldier'*).

> 'O Soldier, Soldier,
> Will you marry me now,
> With a hey and a ho
> And a fife and a drum . . .'

CHARLIE SCUFFHAM'S VOICE (*from off-screen*). Mary . . .
Mary! Have you gone to bed, Mary?
(*She makes no sign of having heard him, although she stops
singing to herself.*)
(*Off-screen, calling louder.*) I say have you gone to bed?
There's Mrs Parker just come visiting. I say Mrs Parker's
here to see you, Mary: are you coming down? Mary!

With a sudden blow she sweeps her soldier on to the floor.

The living-kitchen.
*This is a large room opening direct on to the street. It contains a
kitchen range, table, chairs, sideboard, etc., and is somewhat over-
crowded. The window looks out into the dark street beside the front
door. In the back wall of the room, opposite the front door, are two
other doors: one leading into a scullery-wash-house, and the other
to the base of the stairs.*
CHARLIE SCUFFHAM *stands at the stair door, calling upwards.
He is about sixty, in braces and shirtsleeves – a long lantern-jawed
man, melancholy, and wears steel-rimmed spectacles.*

SCUFFHAM. Mary!
(*He turns back into the room, to confront his wife and* MRS
PARKER. MRS SCUFFHAM *is a large slatternly sentimental*

woman with a generally bothered air. Her friend is angular and sharp of speech, with a certain malicious quality of mind. She is the smarter dressed of the pair, and carries a handbag.) She's not coming down.

MRS PARKER. Gone to bed, has she?

SCUFFHAM. Gone to her room.

MRS PARKER (*significantly*). Ah.

MRS SCUFFHAM. She's perhaps feeling poorly, poor love. She didn't eat her tea.

SCUFFHAM (*sharply*). She never eats her tea.

MRS SCUFFHAM (*injured*). Well, it wor a lovely tea, I made her a lovely tea. There was chips from around the corner, and a bit of pork-pie fried, and treacle we had, and a lovely yellow cake bought special, and she wouldn't take a bite. It's downright criminal, all that good shop food goes to waste. Of course, she thinks on Tommy, all the time.

MRS PARKER. Well, she's only herself to thank for that.

MRS SCUFFHAM (*vaguely compassionate*). She wor always very fond of our Tommy.

SCUFFHAM (*bitterly*). Mrs Parker's right. She's only herself to thank. Them as takes up sword has to perish by sword. When he went for a Regular soldier, he threw up everything I tried to learn him. It's what your husband says, Mrs Parker, Force and Colonialism: that's how he stands now: and strike-breaking and all that. I ask you, is it surprising he got married to . . .

He gestures contemptuously upstairs.

MRS PARKER. Irish, they said she was.

SCUFFHAM (*darkly*). Aye, but *we* reckon there's more to it than that, you know.

MRS SCUFFHAM. Many's the time I've looked at her and wondered.

MRS PARKER (*producing a bundle of tracts*). I thought I'd bring these for her tonight, but if she's gone up to bed . . .

MRS SCUFFHAM (*more to herself than otherwise*). His first leave from the Army, 'Hello, Mum,' he says – 'What do you think of the uniform, Scotch tartan and all – and what do you think of my Mary: we got married last week,' he says. His first leave – 'We got married last week,' he says.

MRS PARKER. It's – like – half a dozen tracts I got from Chapel, if she could be brought to have a read of them –

MRS SCUFFHAM. His first leave it was: he fetches her home, he took her and put her upstairs in the little bedroom, next morning he goes off to Germany and we never hear a word of him since.

SCUFFHAM. She won't read them, Mrs Parker, and that's nowt but bare truth. I've talked myself into lockjaw telling her about the Wrath to Come and where she'll end up if she goes on and where has it got me?

MRS PARKER. She never comes to Chapel.

MRS SCUFFHAM (*mournfully*). I don't understand it. We've tried to get her to change and to go for *proper* religion, but . . .

SCUFFHAM (*hopelessly*). It's – like – Irish, you see, that's what they say she is.

Someone knocks loudly on the street door. As they turn towards the door, the lower sash of the window is thrust up from outside and the SOLDIER'S *head appears.*

SOLDIER. Are you at home? There's someone knocking at your door.

SCUFFHAM (*almost too astonished to speak*). Here, who do you think you are . . .

More knocking.

SOLDIER. Well, have ye no mind to see who it is?

MRS PARKER *opens the front door, very dubiously. Her husband is revealed on the step. At the sight of his wife he looks a little sheepish.*

PARKER. It's all right, Alice, it's me.

MRS PARKER (*dour*). Why?

SCUFFHAM. Hello, Joe. But who . . .

PARKER (*coming in, and indicating* SOLDIER). I met him down the road. I brought him along. Aldershot he ought to be at, but he was misdirected – like.

MRS PARKER *shuts the door.*

SOLDIER. 'Cause of inadequate co-ordination between supply and demand: What d'ye lack, mucker? We havena got it. What, not a sandwich? No! Do ye intend to invite me inside, or are we to be acquainted only through the window like a dram sold after hours? Because it's a piece cold on this pavement-stone.

PARKER. Oh, come in, come in, Serjeant.

(*He goes to open the door. Before he does so he turns and whispers confidentially to the others.*)

Call him Serjeant when he's in – he's not the softest feller to talk to, but he's worth it, you know.

(*He opens the door, and brings in the* SOLDIER. *Very genial.*)

Well, here he is. Serjeant, meet them all: here's Charlie Scuffham and here's our Ida, and this here's . . .

SOLDIER (*with appalling gallantry*). Ye do not need to tell me. She has the very flare and splendour of your nostrils, man. She is your own most faithful wife or I catch badgers in the moonlight. Mistress Parker, your continual health is my eternal solace. And the same to the lot of yous.

He sits down in SCUFFHAM'S *armchair, sprawls out his legs and stares at the ceiling.*

SCUFFHAM. Now, look here, Joe, what's all this about . . .

MRS SCUFFHAM. Who does he think he is, marching into our house?

} (*Together.*)

MRS PARKER. I hope you've some reason for all this, Joe Parker . . .

When they realize they are all talking at once they break off
in embarrassment. There is a pause, then they all speak at
once again.

SCUFFHAM. But what . . .
MRS SCUFFHAM. Who . . .   } (*Together.*)
MRS PARKER. I say . . .

Another awkward pause.

PARKER (*very significantly*). Caledonian Fusiliers.
SCUFFHAM. Caledonian . . .
MRS SCUFFHAM. Caledonian . . .
MRS PARKER. Oh. Oh.

It sinks in, and they speak one after another in great hurry.

SCUFFHAM. Do you mean to say . . .
MRS SCUFFHAM. You mean to say he *knows* summat . . .
SCUFFHAM. Summat of that lad . . .
MRS SCUFFHAM. Our Tommy, he's not got word of our
Tommy?

They all look at the SOLDIER, *who appears to have gone to*
sleep. At length he realizes that this is his cue.

SOLDIER. Ah, he was the boy. Johnny.
PARKER. Tommy.
SOLDIER (*pulling himself together*).
          Scuffham. Ach, he was the boy.
          Tommy Scuffham. *I* was there, aye,
          The day they threw him inside:
          It's at gate of the camp, ye see,
          Half past twelve is midnight,
          Here he comes, wee Tommy,
          Dancing like an ostrich,
          Hooting stinking drunk,
          And five of these Kraut women,

> Bully brawney ten-ton Frauleins . . .
> They comb their hair with razors, those!
> So here's Big McCluskey,
> Serjeant of the Guard
> Who goes there, he says.
> Friend, says wee Tommy.
> Man, I'm no a man
> To kick the teeth in of a friend,
> So he kicks him in the wame.

SCUFFHAM. Who kicks who?

SOLDIER. He kicks him.

SCUFFHAM. Who?

SOLDIER. Why, Big McCluskey, who else?

MRS SCUFFHAM (*in horror*). He kicks our Tommy . . .

SOLDIER.

> Na na na,
> How the devil can he,
> He's bang on his back in the road
> Flatter than a cowpat
> And (God he's the boy)
> He sets his bully foot
> Plank on his thick red neck:
> Hoot, he says, I've killed him.

PARKER (*bewildered*). Tommy Scuffham killed him? He went and killed a Serjeant!

SOLDIER. Have I not just said so? Ye're all as deaf as white herrings. Mphm.

PARKER. But – but – what happened?

SOLDIER. Happened when?

PARKER. Well happened to Tommy, after all that.

SOLDIER. Och aye, to Tommy. Aye well, what happened? Well, what d'ye think *should* happen? They threw him inside.

MRS SCUFFHAM (*tremulously*). Inside?

SOLDIER. Aye. I doubt he's still there.

MRS SCUFFHAM. Not – not in . . .

SCUFFHAM. You don't mean he's gone to *prison*?

SOLDIER. Where else would he go? Aye, aye, the glasshouse.
He broke McCluskey's jaw – put him off duty three months.
I told ye, quite killed.
They all sit stunned.

MRS PARKER (*savouring the situation*). Eh, think of that now.
Prison.

MARY'S *bedroom.*
*She is sitting cross-legged on her bed, tying knots in a woven belt
of the Irish type. Her soldier lies where she has left it in the
previous scene.*

MARY (*in a crooning voice as though repeating a nursery rhyme
or a charm*).
    One year comes and turns its back.
(*Ties knot.*)
    Two years comes and turns its back.
(*Ties knot.*)
    Three years coming.
(*Begins third knot, but leaves it loose.*)
    How to speak
    Words of life are white or black
    But how should I know how to speak?
    For live words now this jaw would break.

The SOLDIER'S *whistle is heard off; playing 'Soldier, Soldier'.
She stiffens into attention, then gets up from the bed, goes to the
door to listen, and hums the tune herself in company with his
music.*

SOLDIER (*calling from off-screen*). Mary, is it Mary, Tommy's
Mary? Oo hoo hoo!

She pulls the third knot tight.

MARY (*to herself*). Three years coming. How to speak.

She turns the handle of the door to open it.

The stairs seen from a point about half-way down.
The door of MARY'S *room is, as it were, above and behind the*
camera, which is looking down at the SOLDIER, *who has come*
out of the living-kitchen and is starting to climb.

SOLDIER. Oo hoo hoo – Mary.

MARY (*off-screen*). Who are you? What do you want?

SOLDIER (*easily*). Not a thing more than one sandwich, egg,
cheese, or meat.

   MRS SCUFFHAM *appears at the bottom of the stairs behind*
   the SOLDIER.

MRS SCUFFHAM. Come down, Mary, do. He's brought us
word of Tommy.

SOLDIER. Ach, he was the boy.

MARY (*coming into the camera range*).
      If it's only a sandwich, mister,
      It'll not take a minute to make.

The street containing the SCUFFHAMS' *house. A typical street*
in a colliery town, with houses of black brick or stone, stone-sett
paving, a general air of muck without much money. It is Sunday
morning. Church bells are ringing. CHARLIE SCUFFHAM
appears at his front door, in shirtsleeves as before. He walks across
the street to a little newsagent's shop, from which he almost
immediately reappears with a number of newspapers. He glances
doubtfully at the front pages of these, then re-enters his house,
picking up a milk bottle on the way in.

The living-kitchen.

CHARLIE SCUFFHAM *comes in from the street, puts his milk and papers down on the table, and studies the papers with an increasing frown. They are all journals of the sex-and-scandal variety with pin-up photographs much in evidence.* MARY *is beside the kitchen range, arranging a breakfast tray. The room is in a very untidy state, as before; but this is increased by the fact that there has been a bed made up on an uncomfortable arrangement of chairs and sofa in one corner.* MARY *turns away from the range, about to carry her tray upstairs.*

SCUFFHAM (*sharply*). What's all that you're carrying ?

MARY (*dully*). Breakfast, that's what.

SCUFFHAM. Who for ?

MARY. Himself upstairs. In your bedroom.

SCUFFHAM (*fussily*). Well, make sure you give him right plenty. How many eggs ? Two ? He could eat three, you know; he's a big strong-set man . . .

MARY. There's no more than two in the house. Oo, it's a lot for him, is two.

SCUFFHAM (*handing her all the newspapers*). Here's his Sunday papers like he said; now you take 'em up.

MARY. I will. Are you wanting a look at them, Mr Scuffham, first ?

SCUFFHAM (*shocked*). Indeed I'm not. Now, is there owt else he'd like ? Must make sure he gets everything he'd like . . .

MARY (*muttering into the breakfast tray*). How about a hug and a kiss of your own wife, or maybe a . . .

SCUFFHAM (*very angry, but not quite sure he heard*). What did you say! Now, you look here, I'm telling you . . .

MRS SCUFFHAM *is seen appearing at the scullery door.*

MRS SCUFFHAM. You take that tray up to the Serjeant, Mary,

and don't talk back to your dad. You ought to show a sight
more grateful, you ought, all the help he's going to give us
for poor Tommy in his trouble.

MARY (*quietly*). I'm sorry indeed. Of course, it's quite right
we should look after the Serjeant for whatever length of
time he's wanting to stay.

MARY *goes upstairs with the tray.* MRS SCUFFHAM *starts
tidying the makeshift bed in a half-hearted sort of fashion.*

MRS SCUFFHAM. Well, it *is* a length of time, you know, choose
what. After all, it'll be near on for a week . . .

SCUFFHAM (*firmly*). Joe Parker says we've to let him lie.

MRS SCUFFHAM (*crossly*). Oh, Joe Parker . . .

SCUFFHAM (*convincing himself as much as her*). Say he goes
back to barracks: they run him in – he's overstayed his
leave. What sort of help can he do for our Tommy's trouble
then ?

MRS SCUFFHAM (*still doubtful*). That's what Joe says.

SCUFFHAM. Aye. But *I* don't know: all them magazine-books
he wants, and Sunday papers, too.

MRS SCUFFHAM. I wish I could follow what Joe Parker was
after.

SCUFFHAM (*pursuing his own line of thought*). Bare women and
that. It's not what I'm used to.

MRS SCUFFHAM. How much money does that Serjeant reckon
we'll need ?

SCUFFHAM. Are we going to chapel ? No, Joe might come
round.

MRS SCUFFHAM. I think I'll go. I feel that upset, a bit of
hymn-singing'd do me good maybe. I'll go with Alice Parker.

SCUFFHAM. Of course, some of them are wearing – like –
camisoles and bathing-dresses : aye. Never mind for money.
We'll pay what's needful.

MRS SCUFFHAM. Army or no Army, Tommy's our lad, he's
our boy.

The SCUFFHAMS' *bedroom.*
This room is rather larger than MARY'S, *but is furnished in*
similar style. It has a brass double bed, in which the SOLDIER *is*
seated, very much at ease, eating his breakfast and studying the
Sunday papers. He is wearing his underclothing. MARY *stands*
beside the bed and watches him eat.

MARY (*rather unfriendly*). There's two eggs for you. There's
     fried bacon, there's toasted bread and marge and jam.
     They'll not be giving Tommy Scuffham that in the
     prison.
SOLDIER (*speaking laconically between mouthfuls*). A half-piece
     stale bread, a cat's-claw lard, a drain-and-a-quarter bracken-
     water and that they call it tea. 'Any complaints?' 'No com-
     plaints, sir.' 'Prisoners, carry on.'
MARY. Justly or unjustly there?
SOLDIER (*pointing out a photo in his paper*).
          Will ye take a look at *her*,
          There's a lifty leg
          Ye could get between ten fingers,
          There's a rump-end for ye . . .
          Full moon over Sandy's haystack, hey?
          Unjustly, what else?
          Did I not make it clear:
          Whatever poor dog of a soldier
          Went *justly* to the jail?
MARY.
          But the two of them below there,
          All that money they're after gathering,
          How will that help?
SOLDIER (*like a cross-examining counsel*).
          Is he or is he not
          To have a retrial?

MARY.

> That's your advice, indeed,
> Why shouldn't it be good?

SOLDIER.

> And how can he have a retrial
> Without there's new evidence?

MARY (*considering slowly*).

> Sure that was your point of view.
> Truly, truly . . .

SOLDIER.

> And how can ye get evidence
> Without that ye pay for it?
> Is he in Germany? He is.
> And what like are the German women?

MARY (*carefully repeating what she has heard*).

> Swear away their grandpas' lives
> For the price of a fish-hook.

SOLDIER (*in some astonishment*).

> That's what I telled ye.
> Ye remember it well.

  (*He points to another photo in the paper.*)

> Ye see her, lassie, ye see her?
> Now what would ye say
> She was wearing under that sweater?
> Ye'll never make me believe
> That's her own unaided effort.

MARY (*with an unexpected satirical smile, her first*).

> His Mum and Dad, you know,
> I'll tell you what I think there:
> I think they're nothing but a pair
> Of washbowls on the waves of ocean,
> They've not I think between them
> Got one notion.

SOLDIER (*acutely*). And who *has* got the one notion?
MARY (*serious again*).

Yourself maybe, why not?
Or what about Joe Parker.

SOLDIER.

Aha there, he's the boy.
Nosey knows
What Nosey ought to know.
Give him the money,
Says Nosey Joe.
Now why?

MARY. He's a good friend of Charlie Scuffham.

The SOLDIER, *having finished his breakfast, pushes the tray away, lays down his newspapers, and gives* MARY *a considering look.*

SOLDIER. And I was a good friend of your Tommy's, was I no? Ach, he says to me one time: 'You ever go to England, mucker, and ye'll stand in the road and ye'll see her come toward ye, and tripping her legs together like the tick-tock of a clock, and she carries her wee belly like the flourishing colours of the regiment, and her brisk bosom, mucker, is a bugle. And then, mucker,' he says, 'ye'll be looking at my wife.' He says that to me.

MARY (*round-eyed*). Truly?

SOLDIER. Aye, truly.

MARY. In Germany, why not.

There is a knocking at the front door, off.

PARKER (*off-screen*). Hello, Charlie, are you in?

SOLDIER. Do we hear Nosey Parker down the stairs?

MARY. I've got to go now, else I'd be late.

(*She walks to the door, then stops, considers, looks at her legs and up at the* SOLDIER *again, with her smile briefly reappearing.*)

Tick-tock, like a clock?

SOLDIER. Tick-tock.

He makes a noise like a bugle.

The living-kitchen.

SCUFFHAM, *alone in the room, opens the door and admits* PARKER.

SCUFFHAM. Come in, Joe, come in. I were just waiting on you. Ida's gone to chapel.

PARKER (*coming in*). Aye. With my Alice. I tell you, Charlie, I could do with a . . .

He makes a gesture suggestive of pouring out and swallowing a drink.

SCUFFHAM (*sternly*). No, Joe, it wouldn't be right. 'Strong drink is raging.'

PARKER. Not in this house it never is.

(MARY *comes in from the stairs, putting on a headscarf. She walks across the room and goes out into the street.*)

Where's *she* off to so swift and airy?

SCUFFHAM (*sourly*). Babylon.

PARKER. Where?

SCUFFHAM. House of Rimmon. No two words for it.

PARKER. How's she been taking the news?

SCUFFHAM. Why, you can't say she's been taking it at all. No effect at all. It fair beats me.

PARKER. Ah . . . I'll tell you what's beating *me*, Charlie, and it's this: if your lad was into an Army jail, why warn't you notified? Next of kin, you know. Or else Mary is, choose what. *She* should have been told.

SCUFFHAM. Maybe we were told. I don't know.

PARKER. What do you mean, you don't know?

SCUFFHAM (*resentfully*). Well, we get these letters, you see.

One month or another month we'll get 'em. Majesty's Service. *I* don't read 'em.

PARKER. Why not?

SCUFFHAM. Well it's not right to trouble a man with that sort of thing. I've got better thoughts to bother with. And Ida don't read 'em either. Why should she? It's only – like – Government Propaganda.

PARKER. Aye, that's a point there. What about Mary?

SCUFFHAM. Oh, *she* don't get no letters.

PARKER. Any Army marriage allowance?

SCUFFHAM. No. I don't reckon our Tommy can have told about her to the Army. Why should he? It's nowt to do with them.

PARKER (*sitting comfortable at the table*). Now look here, Charlie, I've been settling my mind on to this business for a good long while. And this is what it seems to me. Tabulated conclusion: One: Your lad's been put in jail for summat he didn't do or if he *did* do there was extenuating circumstances as was not yet fully brought out. Two: In order to bring them out we are entirely dependent on the good nature of that feller upstairs and you've got to find the money yourself to pay for the witnesses. Three: It can't have been a fair trial if all that is like it is. Four: Why didn't the Army tell you? You say you might have had letters: so what? Because *I* say, Five: It's their business to make sure you *read* 'em. All right, so what does it add up to?

SCUFFHAM (*thinking carefully*). Well, to my way of thought, Joe, it is not all what I'd call democracy. That's right, isn't it?

PARKER. That's right. And I'm going to make a fair commotion about it and all, I'm telling you. There's council elections next month. You know I'm standing, don't you?

SCUFFHAM. Aye. Aye, I know.

PARKER. Aye, well. Here's my platform: ledged, braced, and battened for me. You've always heard my views about jack-booted militarism. Here is the proof.

The SOLDIER *off-screen. Sings. Air: 'Onward Christian Soldiers'.*

SOLDIER.

'Lloyd George knew my father,

My father knew Lloyd George . . .'

(*The* SOLDIER *enters from the stairs in vest and trews, brandishing a cut-throat razor and a shaving-brush.*)

I'm awa' into the scullery for a shave. Which one of yous has any objections?

SCUFFHAM (*nervously*). No – no one of us at all, Serjeant; you carry on. You know where the towel is and the piece of soap, don't you? I wor just going to have a bit of a rinse, myself, but . . .

The SOLDIER *goes into the scullery, singing as before. The other two continue their conversation in abated tones.*

PARKER. Jackbooted militarism. Do you know what that poor lad told me, Charlie? The things that they're going to do to him when he gets back from being late off leave? Fair makes your blood run cold. And for why? 'Cause he missed his train, that's all.

The SOLDIER *sticks a belathered face round the scullery door.*

SOLDIER. Ye know, I'll tell ye a thing, Mr Parker. All women in this world is divided into the two kinds. There's Birds, and there's Puddings. Now of what kind would ye imagine is you wife, man?

PARKER. Eh, I don't know.

SOLDIER. Bird. All sinews and claw feet with a wee bit beak at the north end.

He goes back into the scullery.

PARKER. Now, that's what I like about that feller. Despite it all in the circumstances of his degraded way of life, he still keeps live and smiling.

The SOLDIER *reappears, using the razor.*

SOLDIER. Mistress *Scuffham*: ha! She is, without doubt, a Pudding. There was something of a deficiency in the baking-powder, fell a piece sodden in the oven, did it no? But let that rest. They tell me, Mr Parker, that ye are a sort of a politician. Do ye ken what they think of politicians in the Army?

PARKER. Can't say as I do.

SOLDIER. I'll whisper it. I doubt Mr Scuffham wouldna care to hear it aloud.

He whispers in PARKER'S *ear.* PARKER *jumps to his feet angrily.*

PARKER. Now, you look here, a joke's a joke . . .

SOLDIER. I'll not deny that, mucker.

They glare at each other for a moment. Then PARKER *thinks the better of it and sits down again.*

PARKER. Well, all right, all right, no offence taken.

SCUFFHAM (*anxiously changing the subject*). About that money, Serjeant. We're getting it together, by degrees – like. About how much do you reckon we'll need?

SOLDIER (*cruelly casual*). I wouldna like to say . . . Anything less of fifty they'll spit in your gob.

SCUFFHAM. Eh dear. We can maybe make forty-five if we take out Ida's Post Office . . .

SOLDIER (*helping himself to a draught from the milk bottle*). There's one variety of a woman, ye do not commonly meet her, she is able to combine the qualities both of Bird and of Pudding. She has the wee nervousness of the one and the warmth and fullness of the other. Rare; desirable; she'll load ye down to death.

PARKER. She seems a kind of a pigeon-pie, eh? Heh heh.

SOLDIER. Mphm.

He goes back into the scullery.

PARKER. What I've been thinking, Charlie, you see, not only your Tommy, but *him* as well.

SCUFFHAM. Him?

PARKER. Victim. Jackboots; so forth, so forth. Very good material for a platform, that lad. All them tales he tells . . . why, do you know what he says some of the Army was doing in West Germany a year or two since?

SCUFFHAM. I was here when he told. Fair shocking, warn't it?

PARKER. You see the line, eh? Connived at by Government – like – excesses of military power. Etcetera, so forth. I think he'd do it, you know. And another thing. He's missed his ten-o'clock train. So he might as well stay. What about it?

SCUFFHAM. I don't know . . .

PARKER (*calling*). Serjeant?

SOLDIER (*from inside the scullery*). Hello there!

PARKER. Speaking quite frank, Serjeant, from the shoulder, no holds barred: what is your opinion of the Army?

There is a pause. The SOLDIER *comes out of the scullery, shaved.*

SOLDIER. Will ye ask that again?

PARKER. What is your opinion of the Army?

SOLDIER. I think I'd best to whisper *that* one, too.

He comes forward again to PARKER'S *ear, but* PARKER *gets up and forestalls him with a triumphant smile.*

PARKER. Say no more, Serjeant, say no more. You've told me all I want to know.

The exterior of a typical Nonconformist chapel, very hard, unsympathetic architecture.
Sounds of congregation inside concluding a hymn with a vigorous 'Amen'.

MRS SCUFFHAM *and* MRS PARKER *come out, before the singing stops.*

The chapel porch.
MRS SCUFFHAM *and* MRS PARKER *walk away from the doorway towards a seat set along the chapel wall in the sunshine. Another hymn begins in the chapel.*

MRS PARKER (*sympathetically*). Come along here, love, there's a seat. There you are now.
(*She helps* MRS SCUFFHAM *to sit down, and sits down herself.*)
Are you still feeling poorly?
MRS SCUFFHAM. No. No, I'm a bit better now, Alice, now that I've got out into fresh air. It wor just one of my turns, you know. I think it's all this hot weather. Charlie Scuffham reckons it's the atom bombs they . . .
MRS PARKER. Now, don't try and talk so much, love. Just you sit quiet.
MRS SCUFFHAM. It's near on a week now, Alice, and he wants all our savings . . . well, *I* don't know – your Joe says it's all right, it wor Joe brought him after all, and . . . I don't see how our Tommy could ever have done all them dreadful things . . . (*She starts to cry, and fumbles for her handkerchief.*) It's not right they should just lock him up and never let us know. And what about Mary, that's what I say, Alice – what are we to do?
MRS PARKER (*sagely*). Ah, there'll be a strain there, I'll be bound.
MRS SCUFFHAM. If she could only cry a bit – like – it would be better for her, wouldn't it? I say to her, 'It'll do you good', but she won't take notice: I say to her, 'Have a good cry with me, love', but – but she doesn't seem to want to.
MRS PARKER (*censorious*). It's what they want you never know,

that sort. You take Ethel Hopkins for an instance. Her boy, you know, he was in the Air Force in the war, and he went and he got married in Southampton . . . well, I *mean* . . .

MRS SCUFFHAM. Eh dear. Southampton.

MRS PARKER. He brought her home and the next thing he knew she was off to Scarborough with his own brother.

MRS SCUFFHAM. What, him as worked down pit?

MRS PARKER. Aye. That one. She used to sing him a song about it – (*She breaks off and looks sharply down the street.*) Look.

(*The view down the street as seen from the chapel porch.* MARY *is walking briskly along on her way home from mass. As we watch her we hear the conversation of the other two women continuing.*)
A terrible song she used to sing:
(*She renders it in a queer high-pitched chant.*)

> 'Collier-boys gets gold and silver
> Aircraftmen gets nowt but brass:
> I'm away with a bonny collier
> For to be his dancing lass.'

Ethel told me she heard her sing that under her husband's very nose. Aye, and dancing at him, too.

MARY *walks past the chapel without paying them any attention.* MRS PARKER *and* MRS SCUFFHAM *watch* MARY *out of sight.*

MRS SCUFFHAM (*suddenly catching the allusion*). Eh, but, Alice, you don't think . . .

MRS PARKER (*judiciously*). Of course a collier's not a Serjeant, nor a Serjeant's not a collier.

MRS SCUFFHAM (*very troubled*). Charlie Scuffham says your Joe says he's not a right Serjeant at all.

MRS PARKER (*gloating*). I know. Only making it worse, you see.

MRS SCUFFHAM. Eh dear, I never thought of it *that* way. What are we going to do?

MRS PARKER. There's not much you can do, Ida, except keep a sharp eye.

MRS SCUFFHAM. And that's what I'll do, and all. I'll tell you, Alice, I'll do it.

MRS PARKER. Aye, and I'll help you.

MRS SCUFFHAM (*very determined*). I'll do it.

MRS PARKER. I'll do it, too.

The street containing the SCUFFHAMS' *house.* MARY *comes up the street and enters the front door.*

The living-kitchen.

MARY *enters from the street. She stands just inside the door, astonished at what she sees. What she sees is* PARKER *performing a step-dance on the table among a litter of beer bottles, and the* SOLDIER *sprawling (by now fully dressed) in a chair, whistling a jig on his penny-whistle.* SCUFFHAM *is nowhere to be seen. When* PARKER *realizes* MARY *is in the room he stops dancing and climbs down, a trifle embarrassed.*

PARKER. I was just, er – recollecting, as you might have it, er – like – accomplishments of my youth. Heh.

SOLDIER (*appreciatively*).

> It's no so bad, mucker, mind ye,
> No so bad at all.
> Your old age cries up maybe
> From your knee-joints
> Like blood in the gutter,
> But for all that ye have movement.

MARY (*awestruck*). But where's Mr Scuffham?

SOLDIER (*playing a little twirl of music*).

He's in the back scullery.
He doesna approve.
No, says Charlie,
It's profanation of the Sabbath,
Says Charlie.

SCUFFHAM (*from inside the scullery*). It's a fair disgrace and no two words.

SOLDIER.

Ye hear?
The Demon Drink, is what.
And who's the man he had it brought?
Nosey Parker is the man:
He had it brought.

PARKER (*jovially*). Now, wait a minute, fair's fair . . .

MARY. That's a good quaint whistle you have there.

SOLDIER. It is.

MARY *and the* SOLDIER *stand looking one at the other for a moment.*

MARY (*on the spur of the moment*).
You can whistle me
And I will sing.

SOLDIER. What will you sing?

MARY.

Sure you must know it.
It's a very old tune
Derry down, down, down derry down.

PARKER. Eh, Mary, who'd have thought you sang?

MARY (*tartly*).
Supposing I do sing,
What is there wrong?
(*She turns away from* PARKER *and speaks earnestly and deliberately to the* SOLDIER.)
Tell me if this is not
A strong and proper song.

(She starts to sing, in a fierce, harsh voice, giving more emphasis to the meaning of the words than to the music. The SOLDIER *perches himself on the table-edge and accompanies her on the whistle, picking up the tune without difficulty. He joins raucously in the refrain at the end of each verse, as does* PARKER: *Air: 'The Coal-Owner and the Pitman's Wife'.)*

> 'I met my true love
> In the dark of the night:
> The old moon was dead
> And the new gave no light.
> I met my true love
> At the bottom of the town
> Where dark was the houses
> That cover the ground:
> Derry down, down, down derry down.'

SCUFFHAM *comes in from the scullery, black with anger.*

SCUFFHAM. Mary!

No one takes any notice of him.

MARY (*sings*).

> 'He says, "I'm a walking,
> Will you walk with me?
> I'm walking as far
> As the edge of the sea!"
> I followed him so
> Till he came to the strand
> And there a tall steamer
> Was sailing so grand:
> Derry down, down, down derry down.'

SCUFFHAM.

> Mary, I said, Mary!
> What sort of decent married wife
> Do you reckon *you're* acting
> On Lord's Day and all, what's next!

SOLDIER.

> Hold your holiness, mucker,
> She's singing us a song.

MARY (*sings*).

> ' "Oh now I must board her,"
> My true love did cry.
> "I'll come back and love you
> Again ere I die."
> Let him come back tomorrow
> Or in fifty year
> He's the last I will follow
> To Liverpool pier:
> Derry down, down, down derry down.'

She triumphantly pours herself out a glass of beer and swallows it down. Meanwhile MRS SCUFFHAM *and* MRS PARKER *have come in from the street and are standing aghast.*

SOLDIER.

> For Germany the steamers
> Sail out of Harwich.

MARY.

> That's what they told me
> After the marriage.

SCUFFHAM (*trembling with rage*).

> Marriage to a soldier
> Aye, to a soldier.

MRS PARKER (*very vindictive*).

> Well might she call herself
> Married to a soldier.

PARKER (*trying to smooth things over*).

> It's just a bit of a singsong – like –
> They're none so bad, you know, aren't soldiers,
> Only – like – principle behind them that's vicious . . .

MRS PARKER.

> Aye, and an Irish wife

Well might she call herself
Married to a soldier.

MRS SCUFFHAM (*tearfully*).

Married to our Tommy
I don't know what road to look,
Under our very roof, Alice,
I'm that capped with shame,
Married to a soldier.

SOLDIER (*challenging*).

And what is a soldier?
All right, *I'm* a soldier,
So what word is that worth!

MRS SCUFFHAM. Word of shame . . .

MRS PARKER. Aye, shame.

SCUFFHAM. And no two words.

SOLDIER (*with deep feeling*).

So there is the truth . . .
What word's worth then those soldiers
Lives married to a *whoor* . . .
How many weary soldiers
North, south, islands or desert,
They standing there
All in the thrown stones
Or the bombs or the Serjeants-Major:
And where stands their wives?
Lying on their back
In the backends of Birmingham:
That's where *my* wife stood.
I used to have a wife.
For a whole half-year in Africa
I never heard one word.
But the fat woman kept the bakery
Next door to our house,
She wrote, she said:
'I would never interfere', she wrote,

'But was two sailors or a Yankee
Or a black bus-conductor . . .
They came by night and they went by night
And I thought you ought to know.'

PARKER. But wait a minute, Serjeant . . .

SOLDIER (*disregarding him*).

'I thought ye ought to know', she writes,
And *what* does he know:
That in that outlandish standing
There he has to stand,
Three years, five years,
Eighteen years is me . . .

(*He suddenly breaks off and lurches toward the street door,
picking up and putting on his bonnet as he talks: disgusted.*)

Ach I tried to help yous,
But what service does it work . . .
Why don't I go to Cyprus,
Live with Venus,
Roll me over lovely Cyprus,
Call me a Greek or a Turk . . .

*He goes out violently from the house and slams the door behind
him. They all look at one another.*

MRS PARKER. Well, what was all that about?

PARKER. Birmingham?

SCUFFHAM. I've never been to Birmingham in my life.

MRS SCUFFHAM. Then what d'you reckon he . . .

SCUFFHAM.

Shut your old fat face, will you,
I'm fair fed up with the lot.

There is a pause. MRS SCUFFHAM *snivels.* MARY *goes to the
window and looks out after the* SOLDIER.

PARKER. Who's going to call him back? (*Another pause.*) Well,
somebody'll have to go.

MRS PARKER. What about your savings ?

MRS SCUFFHAM. What about our Tommy.

Another pause. Then SCUFFHAM *and* PARKER *get up together.*

SCUFFHAM
PARKER } *(together).* I'll go and get him . . .

They bump into one another on their ways to the door. MARY *is at the door before them.*

MARY *(wearily).*

　　Don't trouble at all.

　　I'm the one to go.

　　I'll bring him back.

SCUFFHAM. Now, you listen to me . . .

MRS SCUFFHAM. I don't think she ought to go . . .

MRS PARKER. Ask for your trouble, ask it.

MARY.

　　Well, I'm going and I'm going,

　　And that's all about it.

　　Good-bye.

She goes out into the street.

MRS PARKER *(to* MRS SCUFFHAM*).*

　　Do I have to say owt more.

　　Are you deaf as well as blind ?

MRS SCUFFHAM. We mustn't let her go.

(She runs to the door and out a pace or two into the street, leaving the door open. SCUFFHAM *starts out after her, and calls from the doorway.)*

　　Mary, you're to come back here!

SCUFFHAM. Mary, I said *Mary !*

The PARKERS *remain inside the room.*

PARKER.

　　Leave her be, leave her be,

　　She'll maybe bring him back.

The pub.
The LANDLORD *and the* DRINKER *of the second scene in conversation across the bar.*

LANDLORD. He must be off his nut.

DRINKER. Of course he's off his nut. He's fair balmy. Sticks his head through window, he says, 'Window-cleaner,' he says. 'I'm come to clean your windows.' Well, my missus she just looks at him. 'Windows,' she says. 'What do you mean windows – it's Sunday afternoon!' We was just setting down to us teas. Windows!

LANDLORD. Fair balmy.

DRINKER. And then he goes on about this soldier. 'Where's he gone with our lad's Mary?' he says. 'Where's the heathen devil gone!' he says. Then he puts his foot through window, so I gets up and knocks him off his ladder. Drive you to drink!

LANDLORD. It's old Nosey Parker, you know. Him and that Jock Fusilier as broke all my glasses. Nosey was in here an hour since. Had I seen his Serjeant? No, I'd not seen his flickering Serjeant again. Poor old Charlie Scuffham.

DRINKER. Jock Fusilier? If it's *that's* the soldier, I've seen him.

LANDLORD. What, this evening?

DRINKER. Aye, this evening. Down by canal. Back of Ellenroyd's glassworks.

LANDLORD. Where there's all them reeds and bushes?

DRINKER. Aye, in there among the old iron.

LANDLORD. Who was he with?
    (*The* DRINKER *lays one finger slyly on his nose and leers.*)
    Not with . . .

DRINKER (*cunning*). Ah, but I didn't see her, you see, so I'm not saying owt. Just a voice, you see, I could hear, but not so as to know.

LANDLORD (*salaciously*). Like – laughing, and that?

DRINKER (*very salaciously*). Aye . . . 'Stop it, I like it' – eh? Heh, heh, heh!

LANDLORD. Poor old Charlie Scuffham.

The streets of the town, early morning, vehicles, people going to work. Factory buzzers.

The street containing the SCUFFHAMS' *house.* SCUFFHAM *comes up the street wheeling a bicycle with a ladder and bucket. He has a rag bandaging his head and looks worn out. He leaves his bicycle in the street and goes into the house with his impedimenta.*

The living-kitchen.

SCUFFHAM *comes pushing through the door and carries his ladder and bucket across the room to dump them in the scullery.* MRS SCUFFHAM *is asleep in a chair, fully dressed. She wakes up.*

SCUFFHAM. Are they back yet?

MRS SCUFFHAM (*very angry*). Where've you been all night?

SCUFFHAM (*hopelessly*). Cleaning windows.

MRS SCUFFHAM. Have you gone mad?

SCUFFHAM. I thought I wor going. That's why I went out with this lot. I had to do summat, Sunday or no. It wor either work or drink.

MRS SCUFFHAM. Are you sure it warn't drink?

SCUFFHAM (*crossly*). Aye, I'm sure, and I wish it had been. Are they back or aren't they?

MRS SCUFFHAM. They aren't.

SCUFFHAM. Where's Joe Parker and his missus?

MRS SCUFFHAM. I don't know.

SCUFFHAM (*imitating her whine, savagely*). 'You don't know!' What is there you *do* know! Can't even bring up a young lad but you've to let him get hisself all embrangled with

murdering soldiers and dancing delilahs and God knows
what else. I tell you, I'm just about . . .

(MARY *comes in from the street. Her manner is quiet and self-
possessed. She seems, however, to be suppressing some strong
emotion.*)

Oh!

*He has forgotten about his bucket and ladder, which now
encumber the room.*

MRS SCUFFHAM. So you've come home!

MARY. I have.

MRS SCUFFHAM. You go to your room, till I'm ready to talk
to you . . .

SCUFFHAM. You set down there. I've summat to say to you . . .

MARY. One at a time, now. I've time for you both.

SCUFFHAM. I said set down there. I've summat . . .

MRS SCUFFHAM. She can go to her room, go to her room. I
can't hardly bring myself to look her in the face . . .

SCUFFHAM (*storming*). Are you going to set down or not?

MRS SCUFFHAM (*half-hysterical*). She's to go to her room!

MARY. God help us!

(*Her eye lights on the* SOLDIER'S *tin whistle, which lies where
he left it on the table. She picks it up thoughtfully.*)

I'll go to my room.

SCUFFHAM. No you don't . . .

MARY. I do, so!

She goes up the stairs. SCUFFHAM *calls after her.*

SCUFFHAM. Here, come back here! What have you done with
that soldier?

MARY (*calling from up the stairs*). You might well ask, Mr
Scuffham, you might well ask indeed.

SCUFFHAM. *I'll* bring her down, *I'll* find the truth . . .

(*There is a knock on the door. He has got tangled with his
ladder, etc.*)

Who's that?

MRS SCUFFHAM. Maybe it's . . .

SCUFFHAM. Well, open it and see.

> MRS SCUFFHAM *opens the door and* PARKER *comes in, very jovial.*

PARKER. Hello, hello, hello, is he back yet, is he back?

SCUFFHAM. No, he's not.

PARKER. Well, he's on his road. I've seen him just now, seen him in Prospect Street . . . (*He sits down and smacks his hands together.*) Now, you listen to me, Charlie. Everything's lovely, it's all arranged. Last night where do you think I've been. I've been to Trades Union Offices up Balaclava Road, and who's there? The Mayor's there.

MRS SCUFFHAM (*impressed*). What, Alderman Butterthwaite?

PARKER. Aye, Cheery Uncle Butterthwaite. Well, *you* know him, Charlie. He's more than just Mayor; he's like Napoleon in this wappentake – Council, committees, unions and all – and he says to me, 'Joe,' he says, 'Joe . . .'

SCUFFHAM (*also impressed*). He called you Joe!

PARKER. He called me Joe. He says, 'Joe, that soldier's worth a mine of black diamonds, in right place. I want our M.P. to meet him,' he says.

MRS SCUFFHAM. Our M.P.

PARKER (*revelling in it*). That's what he said . . . It's my political future, you know: it's made. You'll be saying Councillor Parker soon. Then Alderman. *Then* what?

> *The* SOLDIER *opens the window as before and thrusts his head in.*

SOLDIER.

Then it'll be Doomsday. Hech!
(*He climbs in through the window.*)
I'm climbing in for my breakfast.

> Doomsday's the day, mucker,
> Ye'll see wee maidens swift as lizards
> Running through the town,
> And all the polismen on the corners
> Give them brandy and red roses.
> Hech. That's the day for me, boy.

MRS SCUFFHAM (*appalled*). Did you say breakfast? Did you say breakfast?

SOLDIER. If ye havena got any, it doesna matter. Mr Scuffham, ye've given me twenty pounds already, I havena spent it, here it is – (*He shows the money in his breast-pocket.*) Am I no an honest soldier? But if ye wish to give me more, I think ye'd better let me have it now. Ye see, I've to leave this town. I can bide awa' from the regiment just so long – all right, it's detention. But longer than that, man, I'm for the glasshouse; and what service can I work for Johnny if I'm sharing his stone-cold cell? Tommy. Give me the money the day, I'll awa' off to Aldershot, so with the boys to Germany, then work it, work it, work it: he gets his retrial.

PARKER. Now, Serjeant, I've got a proposition . . .

SOLDIER. Och aye, the politics: ye telled me down the street. Plenty of time for that, now . . . But the money, I should have it this morning.

SCUFFHAM (*sulkily*). I'm not going to give you any money.

SOLDIER (*sharply*). What?

SCUFFHAM (*almost in tears*). I said I'm not going to give it you! I've been a man of chapel all my life, never touched a drop, never swore an oath . . .

MRS SCUFFHAM (*actually in tears*). The things I've done for that girl. All my cast-off dresses she's had, and there was that lovely blue hat with the cherries on: she turned up her nose . . .

SOLDIER (*understanding*).

> Och, is it *that* the gate the waters flow?
> She's of an age to know her mind,

And that's enough for all.
Tommy's Mary's Tommy's Mary:
But Tommy Scuffham's *yours*.

SCUFFHAM. You're getting nowt out of me, Mister Soldier. You can go back to your murdering and your trampling on sovereign rights of independent folk, and your shooting-down of working men in the streets: but as far as this house goes, you're done and you're capped. No two words.

PARKER (*anxiously*). Charlie, you're making a mistake there. He's not that like of a soldier at all . . .

SOLDIER (*urgently*).
And no more is wee Tommy.
Will I tell ye, Mistress Scuffham,
What like of a soldier is *he*:
He's a scrub-neck convict in an Army jail,
With no more sovereign rights to *him*
Than are lost in the dust
Of a pew of your chapel!
Money? Or no money?
Does he have his retrial?

MRS SCUFFHAM. He's got to have that. He's our lad, Charlie Scuffham. You've *got* to pay that money.

SCUFFHAM. I'm not paying owt.

MRS SCUFFHAM (*her voice rising*). You are!

SCUFFHAM. I'm not . . . I tell you I'm not . . . How much does he want?

(*He refuses to look at the* SOLDIER.)

MRS SCUFFHAM (*very hard and hostile*). How much do you want?

SOLDIER (*airily*). No more than ye can manage. Ye mentioned forty-five quid . . .

MRS SCUFFHAM. That wor with my Post Office. I've not had the time to draw it out.

SOLDIER. Then without your Post Office?

MRS SCUFFHAM. Thirteen over the twenty you've already got.

That's right, isn't it? . . . I said thirteen, Charlie Scuffham; is that right or isn't it?

SCUFFHAM (*reluctantly*). It's right.

MRS SCUFFHAM. Get it and give it him and let him go.

(SCUFFHAM *goes into the scullery*.)

(*To the* SOLDIER.) We're going to let you have that money
because it's for our lad, but you're never to come here again.
Not ever. You've done enough hurt to this house . . .

PARKER (*rather bewildered*). Now, Ida, be reasonable. I can't
make out what you're getting at . . .

MRS SCUFFHAM. You mind your business, Nosey Parker;
it's all your fault as it is . . .

PARKER. Here, I say, Ida . . .

MRS SCUFFHAM (*her voice rising very high*). You're the one as
brought him here; you're the one as . . .

The SOLDIER *has been looking for something round the room.*

SOLDIER. Where's my tin whistle?

MRS SCUFFHAM (*startled in midstream*). Eh, what?

SOLDIER. My old tin whistle, Mistress. Left it on this table
yesterday.

MRS SCUFFHAM. Well, it's not here now. And to speak true
I don't care where it is. *I've* not laid a finger.

SOLDIER. *Someone's* laid a finger . . . *I* know what's happened to it . . .

He starts for the stairs.

MRS SCUFFHAM. Here, where are you going?

SCUFFHAM *comes in from the scullery with a dirty jam jar
full of paper money. He, too, tries to intercept the* SOLDIER.

SCUFFHAM. Aye, where are you going? I'm not having you . . .

MRS SCUFFHAM. Not up there!

But the SOLDIER *is too nimble for them, and is already on the
bottom steps. He holds them back with his hand.*

SOLDIER.

Wife, bairns, and rooftree
I may desert:
But my old tin whistle
Stays hooked to my heart.
(*He deftly twitches the handful of money out of* SCUFFHAM'S *jam jar.*)
Down again in one half-minute.

He goes up the stairs.

MARY'S *bedroom.*
She is crouching on the bed with her toy soldier. She has tears on her face. The tin whistle has been laid carefully in front of the madonna. She is running her belt through her fingers and pulling at the knots in it. There are several more than before, and she pulls them all to see that they are tight.

MARY (*crooning*).

Come soldier, Come soldier,
Come soldier, *Come:*
The knots are tied tight
For to call you home.
(*The door is tried, but it is locked. There is a knock on it. Still crooning.*)
Come soldier, Come soldier,
Come soldier, *Come:*
All the soldiers are dead soldiers
And you are alone.

Another knock.

THE SOLDIER'S VOICE. Mary, will ye open the door?
(*She gets up and opens the door. The* SOLDIER *comes in. Business-like.*)
Where's my tin whistle?

MARY. I have not got it.

SOLDIER. Ach aye, ye've got it. Now, give it over here.

MARY (*as though stupidly*). I tell you I have not.

SOLDIER. It's in this room some place. Now where... Aha, so ...

He sees it and moves to get it. MARY *holds him back.*

MARY. No.

SOLDIER. Na, na, na, lassie. That whistle's no for you.

MARY (*still holding him*). Nor for you now. It will stay where it's been given.

SOLDIER (*laughs roughly and sits down on bed*). Hech, this is rank robbery. Ye could be run into the clink.

MARY. Like Tommy.

SOLDIER. Aye, like Tommy. Now, let's have that whistle.

MARY. Or not like Tommy maybe ? Do you know what I think ? I think that Tommy was never in prison at all.

SOLDIER (*sharply*). Ye think that ?

MARY. I think that.

SOLDIER (*looks at her shrewdly*).

> Aye ? . . . Aye, well, now.
> Ye have a very pertinent notion there.
> Just as between two friends, now,
> What more *further* do ye think ?

MARY (*very simply*).

> Or if he is in prison, you see:
> All that money you're asking,
> You'll keep it for yourself
> And not for him at all.
> That's what I think.

The SOLDIER *grins, very broad and slow, all the time looking at her. Suddenly he jumps to his feet and flings open the door.*

The stairs.

The SCUFFHAMS *and* PARKER *are in an undignified huddle*

half-way up the stairs, trying to overhear the conversation, and are apparently moving upstairs by degrees.

SOLDIER (*from off-screen*). Now, why don't yous three bide downstairs. Here's a *private* conversation takes place, awa' below with yous, hoot, hoot!

They retreat, disappointed, into the living-kitchen.

MARY'S *bedroom.*
The SOLDIER *comes in, and locks the door behind him. He has a confident, impudent smile on his face.*

SOLDIER (*satirically*).
     All right, lassie,
     So I'm just a randy chancer
     Hanging on your house
     And swindling your silver?
     You tell me that but I tell *you*
     There's green rushes on canal-side
     Wouldna dream those words was true,
     There's an old rotten barn roof
     At back of the glassworks wall
     Never heard *those* words
     Last evening or last night.
MARY (*dully*).
     Like rainfall or like snow they fall
     Words are black
     Or words are white.
SOLDIER.
     Now you'd say black:
     Last evening, naked white.
MARY (*looking up earnestly*).
     Then they were nothing at all

> You could call: words.
> Whistling and gone
> And leaves you trembling;
> Who knows what birds
> Then flapped across your grave?
> Among the rushes me and you
> I gave and you gave:
> *You* gave too.

SOLDIER (*sombre*). There's nothing left of that.

MARY. The green rushes whistle and preserve.

SOLDIER (*fierce and rough*).

> Preserve for who?
> The piles of rust and junk
> In Ellenroyd's yard?

(*He chants coarsely.*)

> Any old iron, any old iron,
> Here I'm a maid with a back to lie on
> Fetch me a soldier
> Before I'm much older
> For Tommy he's inside
> And my elbows raxing wide –
> All watery-golden
> Like a hoop of the sun . . .

(*He has allowed a certain softness to creep into the last two lines, so he roughens his voice consciously again.*)

But ye see it's done and ended, lassie. So let's have the old tin whistle.

MARY (*suddenly, after a pause*). How much of the money have they given you?

SOLDIER (*startled*). Hech?

MARY (*speaking very quickly*). I know that at least you've the twenty pounds. Have you more than that or what?

SOLDIER (*not catching her drift*). Is it the money?

MARY (*urgently*). But twenty's enough; it doesn't matter for the rest. You took that money because you told them lies, but I tell you no lies: I'm coming with you, soldier, and I'm living with you and that money's my only fortune and we're travelling today.

SOLDIER. Hey?

MARY. What do I care where we live? I've lived *here* two whole years, so Mother-of-God, what place is there I couldn't live . . .

SOLDIER. And what happens to Tommy?

MARY. I have no more life left for Tommy; all of my life is for you.

SOLDIER. Is that so . . .

MARY. I'm telling you no lies, boy.

SOLDIER (*furiously*). Nor I'm telling you none neither! God help us, a soldier's wife. D'ye imagine I've never met ye before, hell's devil eat your feet, woman – I *married* ye in Birmingham nineteen forty-one! I've tickled your pretty wee lugs and chuckled into your armpits in London and Fort George and Glasgow and Düsseldorf and Naples and Sidi Barrani, and ye're worse each time than the last, and it's this bloody time ye're the worst of bloody all.

(*She looks at him stupefied for a moment, and then starts to weep, or, rather, keen: a strange disconcerting moan which startles him considerably.*)

Ach awa' now, ye've no call for greeting: I'm telling ye truth and ye ken it well it's truth . . .

(*She continues to cry. He is nonplussed and irritated.*)

Mphm! And Irish this time, too.

Have they not always said it:

'An Irish wife
And an Irish knife:
Bright and white
And kill your life.'

Or would do, if ye're daft enough to let them. Well, I'll just get my whistle and awa' . . . God help us, will ye hold your noise!

MARY. You will not touch that whistle!

She fiercely prevents him as he reaches for the whistle.

SOLDIER (*trying to be reasonable*). Now, see here, lassie, what for d'ye have to go greeting and roaring like an old wife in a tram-smash. Ach, hearts-of-justice, did I not make it clear enough to ye the last day I was never a man for long companionings! I canna carry ye with me to the Army . . .

MARY. Why not?

SOLDIER (*despairing*). Why not . . .

MARY.

> Why go to the Army at all?
> Why not let's go to Ireland?
> What's the matter with Ireland?

SOLDIER. Ach, for the matter of that, what's the matter with Egypt, except it's full of Egyptians – or Irish, or whatever: or what the hell do *I* care!

> Look, I'm a travelling man now,
> But when I stop travelling, see:
> Here is the Army
> And it's a close house
> And there's square meals a day
> And it's a man's strong life
> Has four measured sides
> Like four forests round one farm
> And no foul weather except
> Is your own: or a war –
> And we'd be *all* of us in a *war* . . .

(*She has stopped weeping to hear him, but now she starts up again. He pulls money from his pocket.*)

Och, what's the use? I'd be talking till Christmas. Here, look, here's half of the twenty – look, look, I'll make it fifteen. *Now* will ye hold your greeting and let me gang in quiet!

MARY (*irrelevantly*). All these knots I tied for you. Pulling you round me so tight.

SOLDIER. All right, then, take the lot of it then – will ye take the whole flaming lot – take *thirty-three* quid and be damned!

He throws the money across her bed.

MARY (*strongly*). No, I will not! To be living with you, sure, I would take it, but to just steal the money from an old fool and his wife and to travel the world so with only stolen money and but one soul to hold it – no, I will not! Use it yourself, man; it's no good to me.

SOLDIER (*sourly*). No good to nobody – what's the bloody use . . .

(*He shovels up some of the money and stuffs it in his pocket, leaving the rest scattered. He turns to the door. With a sudden awkward tenderness.*)

Ye can keep the whistle, keep it: dance yourself a jig, whiles. Hech, ye're a bonny lassie: but I telled ye that, last evening . . . Good-bye to ye so.

He goes out, leaving her sobbing on the bed.
She is still lying on her bed, but no longer sobbing. She gets up slowly, pulls a shabby little suitcase from under the bed, opens it, and starts to pack it with clothes from her chest of drawers. She picks up her soldier and puts it in among the clothes, all anyhow. She takes up the belt, is about to pack it, then stands considering, and fingering the knots in it. With a sudden decision she ties it round her waist. She picks up the tin whistle, with a curious secret smile. She puts it to her lips, and after one or two false notes begins to blow a passable version of 'Soldier, Soldier'.

The living-kitchen.
The SCUFFHAMS *and* PARKER *are clustered at the bottom of the stairs, listening. They hear the* SOLDIER'S *feet descending.*

MRS SCUFFHAM. He's coming down.

SCUFFHAM. Not afore time.

MRS SCUFFHAM. She wor crying and crying.

They move away from the stairs as the SOLDIER *comes into the room. He walks straight through the room to the front door, putting on his bonnet and picking up his swagger-stick as he passes.*

SOLDIER (*in a hectoring manner*). Is my breakfast ready? If not why not? Put it on the hob and I'll eat it when I'm back. *When* am I back? I canna tell ye . . .

He goes out into the street.

PARKER. Eh, Charlie, what *is* all this about?

MRS SCUFFHAM. What are we going to do, Charlie? However will we break it to our Tommy?

SCUFFHAM. Ah, you might well wonder: and no two words . . .

MARY comes into the room, carrying her suitcase and wearing her outdoor clothes.

MARY. Which way did he go?

SCUFFHAM. Which way . . .

PARKER. He went to the left.

MARY. He went to the railway station. Then I go to the right. That goes to the bus station.

MRS SCUFFHAM. But why to the bus . . .

MARY (*with a new, hard confidence*). So I can find my own road. I don't know where to. I don't care at all. Just out: and good-bye. You can tell my little husband, when he finally comes, that I used to love him once. I dare say he'll be glad for it.

She goes out into the street.
There is a violent knocking on the front door.

SCUFFHAM. *Now* what is it? Don't say he's forgotten summat...

He opens the door and MRS PARKER *hurries in.*

MRS PARKER. Is Joe Parker here?

PARKER (*surprised*). Hello, Alice.

MRS PARKER (*grimly*). Hello. I just met that soldier in street. Where's he off to?

(*They shrug their shoulders. She sits down.*)

Eh, let me get my breath . . . Hello, Ida. Was that Mary just went past?

MRS SCUFFHAM. That's right, Alice. I'm glad you've come when you did. We've a lot to tell you, Alice.

MRS PARKER. And I've a lot to tell *you*, and all! By, I've got some bright news for you!

PARKER. What sort of news?

MRS PARKER. Just a minute while I get my breath . . . So it's Joseph Smart Parker, is it, that chuffed-up about finding a soldier to yell 'Down with the Government', for him that he never thought on to ask a few plain questions first!

PARKER (*alarmed*). What are you talking about!

MRS PARKER. I'm talking about you. Eh, you can reckon you're fair lucky to have me at your back in your politics to stop you making yourself a complete public monkey. If ever you're elected, you can thank me first, I'm telling you . . .

MRS SCUFFHAM (*in fear*). Alice . . .

MRS PARKER (*triumphantly*). I said to myself this morning, I said, 'It's time I did some telephoning.' So I did some. And first lot I rang up was the War Office.

PARKER. The War Office!

MRS PARKER. The War Office. And what they told me . . .

The pub. Lunch-time.
There are a fair number of customers, such as we have seen before, but a much more obvious air of conviviality. The hum of chatter is loud and we are not able to distinguish strands of conversation.

A good deal of business is being done at the bar. The tune 'Soldier, Soldier' is being whistled, and we discover that the performer is the SOLDIER, *equipped with a new tin whistle and an admiring circle of drinkers. He finishes the tune with a flourish and there is some applause. He acknowledges this.*

SOLDIER. There's words to it, too. (*He sings.*)
    'O Soldier, Soldier,
    Will ye marry me now,
    With a hey and a ho
    And a fife and drum?'
And then he tells her, ye see:
    'O Lady, Lady,
    I canna marry you –
    Because I have
    No coat to put on.'
And so forth. Has every man a drink? All right, my boys, here's the boy that's paying – (*He addresses the* LANDLORD.) Snap it around mucker; they're all rioting for the drink.

He throws money on the bar counter, and the drinkers cluster in with their orders.

FIRST VOICE. Black-and-tan and a pint of bitter . . .
SECOND VOICE. I'll have a stout.
THIRD VOICE. Stingo for me, Billy . . .
FOURTH VOICE. Stingo and bitter . . .

Etcetera.
The LANDLORD *bustles about, serving them all. The* DRINKER *whom we have met before pushes away from the bar carrying a foaming glass, and sways across in front of the* SOLDIER, *nearly spilling his drink.*

DRINKER (*cheerfully*). Hey, soldier, did he marry the lass after all?

SOLDIER. Ha! He says to her, 'I havena got a coat,' he says. (*Sings*).

> 'So off she went
> To her grandfather's chest
> And she fetched him a coat
> Of the very very best
> Says: "Come on, me brave boy,
> Now put this on." '

(*He breaks off, staring at the door. We see that* PARKER *has just entered, and is looking at the* SOLDIER *in some astonishment*.)

> Hech, it's Mr Parker!
> What'll ye drink, Mr Parker?
> Name it and it's served!

PARKER (*bitterly*). I didn't reckon to find *you* still here.

SOLDIER. Did ye no? Man, I've just bought myself a new tin whistle. I couldna leave this town without I'd tried it out.

PARKER. I think you and me, we'd better have a quiet word.

SOLDIER. Ach, aye, a quiet word. (*To those at the bar*.) I'm awa' to have a word.

He and PARKER *withdraw to a table in the far corner of the room, and sit down.*

PARKER. First I'd better tell you I've been making a few inquiries. This morning after breakfast I rang up the War Office.

SOLDIER (*airily*). Och, imagine.

PARKER (*righteously indignant*). You know what they told me? They told me as Tommy Scuffham warn't in prison at all.

SOLDIER. Then where is he?

PARKER. *They* don't know: *I* don't know. He was discharged medically unfit nine month since. That's the last as anyone's heard. But he's not in prison and he never has been in prison.

SOLDIER (*airily*). Och, imagine.

PARKER (*furiously*). Well then: what about it! You told me . . .

SOLDIER (*contemptuously*). I told ye this: I told ye that. Ye ask daft questions, ye got daft answers. Besides, I was three parts fou. I'll tell ye another thing. I never even heard of Johnny Scuffham before I met you that time.

PARKER. You never even heard . . .

SOLDIER. I'd to keep ye contented somehow. Och, man, d'ye imagine I ken every sock-headed man in the whole regiment?

PARKER (*spluttering*). Why – why – you know, I could get you ten year for this!

SOLDIER. Mphm. For what good that'll do ye . . . I'll tell ye what ye *will* do: ye'll gang up on your platform and ye'll tell your jolly muckers that your poor military victim's gone back to the Army – in manacles and leg-irons, if ye like. Ye might win your election. But tell them anything else, boy, and they'll laugh ye into the canal.

PARKER. What about Charlie Scuffham's money?

SOLDIER (*gesturing towards the crowd at the bar*). Hech, *what* about it? If he gangs and hires a stomach-pump, he'll maybe get his value. But for your own reputation, ye'd be advised to keep him quiet . . . And now you'll forgive me while I catch the afternoon train. If I dinna get to Aldershot the night, I'll be posted a deserter. And then I'd have to ask for forty pound so as to bribe ye for a false witness. (*He rises from the table and finishes his drink in a quick swallow.*) Good day to ye, mucker.

(*He walks toward the street door, calling to the crowd and the* LANDLORD *as he goes.* PARKER *is left sitting open-mouthed at the table.*)

Good day to the lot of yous. There's the money on the timber for drinks for every man.

He walks out of the bar. The engraved glass door swings open and then shuts behind him.

The SOLDIER *strides away from the pub, down the street,*

towards the camera. We see him in long-shot at first.

Then a close-up of his boots swaggering along the pavement stones.
As he walks the drums and fifes come in with 'Soldier, Soldier' and we hear the SOLDIER'S *voice singing the final verse of the song. (Sings.)*

'O Soldier, Soldier,
Will ye marry me now
With a hey and a ho
And a fife and drum.
O Lady, Lady,
How can I marry you
When I have already
A wife of my own?'

Theatre Workshop and Forum

There is a considerable variety of activity possible in connection with these plays. Apart from reading and general investigation of characters and situations, which can be undertaken by groups of any size, each of the plays can be divided into phases for rehearsal (not necessarily with performance in mind) and improvisation purposes. Where large numbers of people are considering small cast plays or scenes, it will usually be found more interesting and advantageous if they are divided into smaller groups each working on the same phase or scene or different groups undertaking different aspects of the play. Even when space is limited, it is possible to have several groups all working at once—and it is surprising how soon concentration and absorption develop to a point at which noise outside any group ceases to be distracting.

Acting any of these plays can be undertaken with the actors moving around with the books in their hands, but it will be usually found more interesting if, after some preliminary reading and discussion has taken place, books are put aside for the acting. The actors then use their own words, keeping as close as possible to the original thought flow and action sequence. This requires *understanding* rather than memory and can follow after any careful examination of the way a scene is developed.

Sometimes further insight into and understanding of a play can be gained by taking a scene closely associated with the characters of the play, but just outside the action as written. Character reactions can be agreed upon, together with the basic structure of the new scene, and then the dialogue can be improvised by those taking part. A preliminary run-through will probably raise many questions which can then be sorted out and clarified in discussion and further rehearsal. If both the scenes from the play and the new scenes are improvised, it will soon be found that the actors are having to understand the playwright's style to remain faithful to his purpose. As the process of improvisation continues, actors will soon discover that:

a they are getting closer and closer to the text—dialogue and eventually (often without conscious effort) they are using the playwright's full text; and

b their own improvisations are capturing the style and approach of the author.

The following ideas stemming from the plays will help to suggest something of the range of topics and ideas inherent in these dramas. They could be approached in any number of ways:

  i as questions to be discussed with close reference to any one or more of the plays;

 ii as discussion material in a wider and more general context;

iii as the basis for building dramatic scenes, improvisations, dance dramas;

iv titles for written work—prose or verse—based on the facts of the plays or incorporating personal ideas and experience.

Mainly about 'There's No Room for You Here for a Start'

1 Describe local council estates from the point of view of plans and planning.
2 Of what is the privet hedge a symbol? What other social symbols do you recognize?
3 Discuss deformity, suspicion and prejudice. How are the concepts related?
4 Do your neighbours follow a predictable behaviour pattern? How do you think they regard you?
5 What is a home? What is a house? What are digs?
6 Do you agree that smoking is 'a dirty stinking habit'? (p. 24). Why?
7 Who is the Town Clerk? Why does he have such power? Discuss how he looks and dresses.
8 What is the point of the Town Council?
9 Discuss different ways of dealing with people—authoritively, persuasively, sweetly, with winning ways, disarmingly.
10 What is a 'perfect gentleman'?
11 Write some examples of official wording and style in letters and communications. How do they link with manner in personal relationships?
12 Discuss jealousy in love relationships. How can you deal with this?
13 What is your attitude towards policemen? Why is this justified?

Suggestions for Improvisations
1 At the council offices—the official reaction before their visit to 'The Farm'—the scene after their first visit and again after their last visit.

2 Various scenes at the police station during different parts of the play.

3 How the gun and the clubs first came into the house and why they were stowed in the attic.

4 Len's leaving home and the scene prior to this with his mother.

5 Meetings between Len and Mary at various times throughout the action of the play.

6 Mary at the hostel; Len at work.

7 The day after the end of the action.

Some Quotations from the Play
which could form the Basis for Further Discussion
or Debate, or Improvised Dramatic Work

LEN. Although your property is not directly the responsibility of the authority, the Council must warn you that you are bound by the by-laws and regulations of the Council, and that your original guarantee of tenure must depend on your compliance with decisions taken by the Council for the benefit of the entire Estate (p. 24).

LEN. Like I always say, I'm funny-looking, but I'm armless. There, that nearly had you smiling (p. 26).

LEN. The rest of it is just writing. Office writing. It says your hedge is too high.
LILY. Too high for what?
LEN. Too high for their liking.
LILY. But what should I do?
LEN. Tell you what, I'll cut it for you. Trim it nicely (p. 28).

LEN. I'm about wild with getting no sleep two mornings, I can tell you, Harold. They got no consideration. Bang, bang, bang on the door, and all this hectoring, questions, questions. It doesn't take two minutes o' that and you got a nasty feeling everyone's against you and somehow it's all your fault. Well, they can just watch out (p. 33).

MARY. Well, he does seem to have made an impression in a week.

LILY. Mary, he's a perfect gentleman (p. 34).

LEN. Now an't I told you? You're very foolish to be frightened. Everybody's frightened these days. I don't understand it. What you got to be frightened *about*? He won't eat you. I've yet to see a cannibal Borough Surveyor. What you got to lose? (p. 40).

LEN. Oh. I slipped up somewhere along the line, I see. I an't going to inquire; no good'll come o' that. It was all meant for the best. You know that, don't you? And I think the world of you. Oh, o' course I said that, didn't I? Like, and I soon shot them off, didn't I? (p. 46).

LEN. That's just what I am! Stupid! That's a big lump o' bone I got there. Solid, right through to the middle. But you don't see me frightened, so now you tell me who's daft (p. 41).

LILY. There's no substitute for parents' love, is there? So anyway I was left . . . raw . . . I felt raw. You know, open (p. 47).

LILY. Some people'd be glad to know and hold it against me; not everybody's like you.

LEN. Oh, they are mostly, I think (p. 48).

LILY. It's just that . . . I've come to love him, Mary, and you mustn't be jealous, because it's very wonderful. I know he's as daft as a brush, but you can't guess how he is with me (p. 49).

Mainly about 'The Kitchen'

1 What is the purpose of work? Is it making money and maintaining a standard of living?

2 How important is it to get on with the people you work with?

3 How far in contemporary society is it possible to find fulfilment in a job? Where it is not possible, what compensations can be found out of working hours?

4 Alfredo 'is the worker and the boss is the boss, and he (Alfredo) probably despises the boss'.

5 Nicholas 'behaves with a wild heartiness, as one who is accepted. And as one who is accepted he imititates'. How important is it for people to feel accepted and by whom? And how relevant are 'acceptance' and 'imitation' to 'with-it' groups and 'in-cliques'?

6 Is the kitchen a man's world?

7 How much truth does there seem to you to be in Wesker's image of industrial society?

8 Ours is said to be a violent society. Do you agree? Are there other reasons for this besides those suggested by Wesker?

9 What do you gather from the play is Wesker's attitude to racial integration? How do you react to it?

10 Max enjoyed his story about the electric chair. Do you relish horrors? Why? And why do people generally?

11 When you take away a man's dignity he is fighting mad.

12 How would you answer Mr. Marango's last speech?

Suggestions for Improvisations

1 Gaston's row with Peter.

2 (a) A head waiter and (b) a head waitress bring a number of customers' complaints.

3 Kevin comes for interview for his job.

4 Try continuing the play. What happens next?

5 **a** The Chef is retiring. It is his last evening of work. (Remember Peter left two or three years before. There may be other staff changes too. Will the remaining characters have changed in any way?) **b** The new Chef's first day.

6 Peter meets:

    a Monique   **b** Kevin   **c** Dimitri
    some months after the end of the play.

Quotations

PETER. Oh, you get good money here—but you work! (p. 94.)
You know your trouble Max? You been here too long. (p. 98.)
It's all money. The world chase money so you chase money too. (p. 108.)
A dream? . . . I can't dream in a kitchen! (p. 138.)

KEVIN. He talks about peace and dreams and when I ask him if I could use his cutting-board to cut me lemons on this morning he told me—get your own. (p. 129.)

PAUL. Nobody knows when to stop. A quarrel starts and it goes on for months. When *one* of them is prepared to apologize so the other doesn't know how to accept—and when someone know how to accept so the other . . . ach! Lunatics! (p. 97.)

ANNE. The poor boy. He's no parents you know. (p. 86.)

MAX. He's a bloody German, a fool, that's what he is. (p. 86.)

NICHOLAS. They should kill 'em off! Kill 'em off! The lot! Boche! I hate them, you know? I don't hate no one like I hate them. And they want to abolish hanging now. You read about it? (p. 109.)

CHEF. Who are you, tell me? In all this big world who are you for Christ's sake? (p. 145.)

DIMITRI. . . . in a factory a man makes a little piece till he becomes a little piece . . . . (p. 89.)

Mainly about 'Soldier, Soldier'

1 What are the ideas you associate with the word 'soldier'?
2 What are mottoes? Discuss the power, force and appeal of rhymes and jingles.
3 What does it mean to be 'absent without leave'? What is the difference between discipline and restriction?
4 What is the appeal of the toy soldier to kids?—to Mary?
5 Distinguish between glamour and glory.
6 What is the power and pull of Chapel? What are Non-conformists and what attitudes do you associate with them?
7 What is a 'con' man and how does he work?
8 Drink and pubs and prejudice—discuss all three separately and any relationship you can see between them.
9 How much stigma is there in having been to jail? What problems does this reveal?
10 Would you take in a stranger? Talk about the differences, similarities and problems seen in accepting Mary and the Soldier.
11 Draw up character studies for each of the folk in this play.
12 'Profanation of the Sabbath'—what is it and what do you feel about the idea?
13 'Nosey Parker.' How did the term originate? What other names have interesting associations? Why?
14 There is often a battle between people and atmospheres of northern towns and southern towns. Why? What characteristics do you associate with each?
15 What are your attitudes towards the institutions of (*a*) marriage (*b*) home (*c*) home town?

Suggestions for Improvisations

1 The Soldier recounting the adventure back at barracks (**a**) to the men (**b**) to the C.O.
2 The scene when Mary first arrived in the house of the Scuffhams.
3 Parker and Scuffham meet the Mayor after the Soldier has left.
4 The ladies at Chapel after the Soldier has left.
5 The pub the day after the play's events.
6 The Scuffham's home; the Parker's home at various other points of the action.
7 Three months later—the Scuffham's son returns.
8 Six months later—the Soldier returns.

Quotations

PARKER. There's no call for discourtesy, you know. I did you a favour getting you out of that public.

SOLDIER. Awa' with your favours.

PARKER. Now then, now then . . .

SOLDIER. I am seeking my own society the night. I need no man's favourings. (p. 167.)

SCUFFHAM. Mrs. Parker's right. She's only herself to thank. Them as takes up sword has to perish by sword. When he went for a Regular soldier, he threw up everything I tried to learn him. It's what your husband says, Mrs. Parker, Force and Colonialism: that's how he stands now: and strike-breaking and all that. I ask you, is it surprising he got married to . . . (p. 172.)

MRS. SCUFFHAM. His first leave it was: he fetches her home, he took her and put her upstairs in the little bedroom, next morning he goes off to Germany and we never hear a word of him since. (p. 173.)

SCUFFHAM. She won't read them, Mrs Parker, and that's nowt but bare truth. I've talked myself into lockjaw telling her about the Wrath to Come and where she'll end up if she goes on and where has it got me? (p. 173.)

MRS. SCUFFHAM. . . . don't talk back to your dad. You ought to show a sight more grateful, you ought, all the help he's going to give us for poor Tommy in his trouble. (p. 180.)

MRS. SCUFFHAM. Army or no Army, Tommy's our lad, he's our boy. (p. 180.)

SOLDIER. Ach, for the matter of that, what's the matter with Egypt, except it's full of Egyptians—or Irish, or whatever: or what the hell do *I* care! (p. 210.)

SOLDIER. I told ye this: I told ye that. Ye ask daft questions, ye got daft answers. Besides, I was three parts fou. I'll tell ye another thing. I never even heard of Johnny Scuffham before I met you that time. (p. 216.)